How to Be a

VODKA
SNOB

How to Be a

VODKA
SNOB

Brittany Jacques

PHOTOS BY Jessica Ebelhar

RED ⚡ LIGHTNING BOOKS

This book is a publication of

RED ⚡ LIGHTNING BOOKS

1320 East 10th Street
Bloomington, Indiana 47405 USA

redlightningbooks.com

This book is printed on acid-free paper.

Manufactured in Korea

First printing 2021

ISBN 978-1-68435-128-2 (hardcover)

This book is dedicated to the "little water" snobs, the enthusiasts, and those who appreciate the subtleties, nuances, and sophistication of vodka. I lift my copper Moscow Mule mug to you in salute.

CONTENTS

Authors' Note

Dear Reader,

Brittany Jacques is the pen name used by my husband and me to write *How to Be a Vodka Snob*. We have a shared passion for vodka, and this book couldn't have been written without both of us. That said, the book is written from my perspective (hi!), and Jay is the name used by my husband in these pages.

Jay and I are not professional mixologists. We love learning about this amazing beverage and hope to share some of the insights, facts, tidbits, and recipes that we have discovered with you.

We've researched this work to the best of our ability. Any mistakes are our own. Explore the further reading recommendations in the back of the book to dive deeper into the history, myths, tales, and lore.

From the bottom of our hearts—*and our Collins glasses!*—we hope you enjoy. Cheers!

The wife half of the Brittany Jacques team

Acknowledgments

First of all, I want to say thank you to my Savior Jesus Christ for allowing me the opportunity to write this book.

Second, I have to thank my husband, Jay. Babe—without your support, this book would have only been a dream left on the shelf . . . *albeit the "top shelf," of course*. Thank you for going on distillery tours with me and, of course, sharing in all the tastings. I love you so much.

To my kids: You are the sweetest, most precious children that a momma could ask for. I love you always. Don't ever grow up.

A big thanks to my parents, who never actually had liquor in the house! I think growing up in a home where alcohol wasn't a part of everyday life let me be more particular about drinking when I got older. Thanks for being so supportive.

To my agent Cyle—thank you for believing in me and in this project. If you ever come down this way, we'll have some berry Cîroc to celebrate, Jacques-style.

To my amazing editor Ashley Runyon—you are one of the most fun and encouraging people to work with. I was nervous about putting together this book, and you put all my anxieties at ease. Here's to hoping we can have a little #VodkaAndChill time in the future.

To my best friend Michelle—thanks for encouraging me when I felt like I wasn't qualified to write about being a vodka snob, although we both know very well that the snobbery grew as a result of writing this. Here's to key lime vodka with ginger beer—#FLMoscowMules for life!

To Sarah H. and Matty G.—you are our faves, and we can't wait for another pool party, so we can break out the yummy snacks and #AlltheDrinks. You both have always been there for our family, and I thank you so much for your support. I love you guys.

To Anna Francis, Stephen Matthew Williams, Nancy Lightfoot, and the rest of the team at IU Press and Red Lightning Books: We appreciate you all so much and are grateful for the opportunity to work with you on this book. It has been an absolute pleasure.

And finally, to my readers—thank you for reading this book. I hope you love the recipes and the fun facts, and I hope that you're able to find your own signature drink. Above all, drink responsibly, drink with sophistication, and let out your inner vodka snob. Поехали! Here we go!

THE NOT-SO-BASIC BASIC BEVERAGE

Not All Vodkas Are Created Equal

Vodka is often the drink of choice at late-night parties, the clear beverage providing the liquid courage needed to show off never-before publicly witnessed dance moves. When cost is the primary deciding factor on which liquor to purchase, the cheapest of cheap vodkas get poured into those red Solo® cups with little thought to how the final drink will taste. Heck, in those circumstances, it doesn't much matter how it tastes.

An underappreciated luxury, vodka is often relegated to the role of a cheap filler beverage to punch up the cola or balance cranberry juice. Yet vodka is more than what it seems. Distill corn and you will get sweet notes; distill from soy and the result will be super smooth and mellow. Distilling from potatoes yields a rather loaded or heavy—sometimes even oily—finish, whereas wheat tends to be one of the more common bases for vodka due to its naturally light return. These subtle notes are all but lost once they're tainted with cola or juices.

The complexities of vodka are not for the rushed or impatient. They are subtle. Smooth. Refined. Vodka's nuances are reserved for the purists, the elites, those who are willing to be labeled as . . . *gasp!* . . . snobs.

This has not always been the case. In the early 1900s, the majority of Americans were snobs when it came to vodka. So snobby, in fact, they didn't care for it at all. In her history "How America Fell in Love with Vodka" for *Gastro Obscura*, Natasha Frost recounts how Smirnoff was able to draw in vodka drinkers using the odorless characteristic as a selling point: it won't leave you with bad breath. *Anyone need an Altoid*? According to Frost, in its early days in America, vodka was utilized in combination with other beverages instead of drinking it straight, so the Screwdriver, Bloody Mary, Ice Pick (iced tea and vodka), and Bull Shot (vodka mixed with beef broth) became the drinks of the day.

Vodka around the World

Vodka's journey to the good ol' United States of America began when the son of Russia's most famous vodka maker was chased out of the country after the Bolsheviks came to power. Vladimir Smirnov settled in France and set up shop, reviving his family's distillation business under his newly styled name Smirnoff. In 1934, Rudolph Kunnett bought the brand and began distilling vodka within the borders of the United States. Kunnett ultimately sold the brand to John G. Martin, who is credited with inventing the Moscow Mule (but more about that in a later chapter).

While vodka is typically distilled from wheat or rye, various wars and famines have forced vodka to be distilled from whatever substance was available. Most Americans have heard stories about the American Prohibition era, but very few have ever heard of the vodka prohibitions in Russia, and it's an interesting tale.

During World War I, Tsar Nicholas II banned vodka sales in Russia to promote order and sobriety, and the ban was continued under Vladimir Lenin. There was no vodka to drink and no vodka to sell. The state revenue lost from vodka sales hit Russia hard as it was fighting World War I.

An unhappy side effect of the vodka prohibitions was that Russians used grain to make moonshine, which produced no tax revenue. All that moonshining also led to food shortages, since grain was being used not only for food, but to create more vodka.

Despite the costs of drunkenness and alcoholism, vodka was a vital part of the country's economy. Walter Moss, in his *History of Russia*, reports that when

Stalin came to power, he made sure enough grain and potatoes were available for vodka production during the famine of the early 1930s, when vodka sales provided one-fifth of the government's revenues.

Despite vodka's role in Russian history, the question of which country invented vodka remains up for debate, with both Russia and Poland claiming to be originators of this prized liquor. But it is Russian chemist Dmitri Mendeleev, the inventor of the periodic table, who is credited with creating the "perfect formula" for vodka. Whether you're on Team Russia or Team Poland, the fact is uncontested that in its beginning stages, vodka was a crudely distilled medicinal liquor estimated to contain less than 14 percent alcohol by volume (abv). For comparison, vodka in America is now at least 40 percent abv (also known as 80-proof).

> ## Fun Fact
>
> The Russian department at Macalester College lists a variety of traditional names for vodka, including bread wine, bitter wine, burning wine, hot water, the monopolka, crankshaft, the white stuff, and the bitter stuff.

What Is Vodka Made From?

As a vodka snob, it's important to understand the vodka basics, like the different ingredients that vodka is made from, the process of distillation, and the flavoring techniques that give this beautiful drink its various mouthfeels and tastes.

Vodka can be made from anything that yeast will eat. The majority of vodkas are made from soy, corn, rye, wheat, potatoes, sweet potatoes, cactus, whey, pears, grapes, barley, milk whey, or a mix or blend.

The purpose of distilling is to remove the flavor of the base ingredient until the liquid is neutral, meaning it has no flavor trace of the original material. Unlike whiskey or bourbon, vodka is not aged or colored in any way, and it is generally distilled more times than other liquors. Generally speaking, vodka

will be distilled at least three times to ensure that it is a pure vodka. Several distilleries will distill five times, and some even go as high as ten times. Each additional distillation process yields a cleaner, purer liquor.

A benefit of vodka's ability to be made from different bases is that people with sensitivity to gluten can avoid it completely by choosing a vodka made from potatoes or corn. A list of some top gluten-free vodka brands to get you started was put together by Charlotte Chilton of *Town and Country Magazine*, including Tito's, Crystal Head Vodka, Ciroc, Grey Goose, Dixie, and Boyd & Blair Potato Vodka.

Ingredients Matter

In an interview with Ross Scarano at *Complex*, Claire Smith-Warner, head of Spirit Creation and Mixology at Belvedere, says that good vodkas aren't tasteless, but rather full of flavor and aroma. This is due to the quality of ingredients, and the end result should have the personality of what the vodka was distilled from.

The texture of vodka is also important, especially if you're participating in a tasting. When a vodka is chilled, the texture changes. It becomes richer and coats the inside of your mouth. As Smith-Warner tells Scarano, "Find a sweet spot—at Belvedere, that's around 48 degrees Fahrenheit—then you'll have the cold, the weight, the viscosity, but still have the lovely characteristic of the grain coming through."

The idea that vodka is boring or simply an elevated version of rubbing alcohol is a tired and silly notion to the true connoisseur. There are incredible and talented vodka distillers that take the time and use only the finest ingredients to produce an exceptional product.

Ingredients matter for a number of reasons. Vodka is great for low-carb dieters, and many brands are safe for those who need a gluten-free spirit. However, as Green Hope, purveyors of organic vodka point out, when looking at labels, it can be hard to figure out what exactly is in the vodka and where those ingredients are sourced, since the ingredient list is often limited to the base of the vodka and a note about whether there are artificial ingredients or not.

When counting calories, it's the extra syrups and mixes that can cause blood-sugar spikes. Look for vodkas that are free of artificial flavorings but are infused with high-quality ingredients that deliver an amazing, rich taste. So if you want to indulge in some fun buttered-popcorn or peanut-butter-and-jelly flavored vodkas, hold your head up high and sip away!

Distillation

The distillation process removes impurities from the vodka. While many will write off vodka as "odorless and tasteless," that's not always the case. Without proper distillation, impurities can be left behind that actually do affect the taste. But that doesn't mean that the number of times a vodka is distilled is proportionate to the quality. The truth is, distilling the *right* number of times is the important factor, and that number is dependent on the raw materials the vodka was made from.

The term *heat* refers to the burn in the throat or on the back of the tongue after swallowing straight vodka and can help determine the smoothness level of the vodka. In fact, the quality of the vodka matters more than the taste. A study by Damaris Rohsenow and her colleagues from Brown University found people who drink purer alcohol may feel fewer bad effects after drinking than people who drink alcohol with more impurities.

Brands by Base Ingredient

I wanted to showcase some brands of vodka by categorizing them by their base ingredient. This is just a quick guide compiled from my experience and a variety of online sources and not an exhaustive list. If you don't see your favorite vodka listed, it is in no way a slight against that brand.

WHEAT VODKAS

Characteristics

Light, crisp, clean, sweet

Notes of fresh citrus

Needs less distilling because wheat is delicate (typically not more than three times)

Brands

Absolut (winter wheat) / Sweden

Chopin (wheat and other single-ingredient vodkas) / Poland

Grey Goose (winter wheat) / France

Ketel One / Netherlands

Pinnacle / France, distributed by Beam, United States

Stolichnaya Elit (wheat and rye) / Russia

Svedka / Sweden

ZYR (winter wheat and rye) / Russia

POTATO VODKAS

Didn't Karen Walker (Megan Mullally's character from *Will & Grace*) have the best one-liners in sitcom history? "You say potato, I say vodka." Her fondness for vodka martinis and inability to care about anything somehow made her endearing and the one some call the true star of the show.

Karen's infamous line opens us up to the beautiful world of non-wheat vodkas, which many believe are more flavorful. Imagine taking a big, delicious bite of creamy mashed potatoes. Vodka made from this root vegetable plays up that oh-so-glorious, heavier mouthfeel. But Crystal Fenton of *Leaf.tv* points out that while some believe the first vodkas were made from potatoes, potato vodka is not an Eastern European tradition, since many potatoes are not able to grow or thrive in a climate with such long periods with frozen ground.

Characteristics
Full, heavy, earthy

Needs more distillation to remove impurities

Brands
Boyd & Blair / United States

Chopin / Poland

Famous / United States

Glacier / United States

Grand Teton / United States

Hammer + Sickle / Russia

Luksusowa / Poland

RWB / Unites States

Schramm Organic / Canada (British Columbia)

Vikingfjord / Norway

Woody Creek / United States

Zodiac / United States

GRAPE VODKAS

Grapes are not just for wine anymore. Grape vodkas are newer to the vodka scene than grains and potatoes, but they seem to be here to stay. Some popular brands distill their vodkas from grapes, so don't be afraid to try one.

Characteristics
"Stemmy" overtones

Fruity mouthfeel

Brands
Bombora / Australia

Cîroc / France

CooranBong / Australia

DiVine / United States

Hangar 1 / United States

Idol / France

Lokka / Turkey

Roth / United States

Swan's Neck / France

CORN VODKAS

Corn vodkas can get a bad rap as the least flavorful vodkas, but some popular brands are made out of corn. For example, my husband often says, "If you can't beat Tito's in price or quality, then you should just quit."

Characteristics
Little taste

Subtle flavor notes (aftertaste)

Brands
Crystal Head (also made with peaches) / Canada

Deep Eddy / United States

Krome / United States

L'Chaim (kosher) / Israel

Smirnoff / multinational

Social House / United States

Tito's / United States

OTHER INGREDIENTS

Some of these brands are blends, made from sugar cane, rice, or other creative ingredients that set their vodkas apart from the competition.

Brands
Belvedere (rye) / Poland

Cayman Blue (sugar cane) / Dominican Republic

Crystal Head and **Iceberg** (peaches-and-cream corn) / Canada

Effen (rye) / United States, but distilled in the Netherlands

Finlandia (barley) / Finland

Han (barley and rice) / South Korea

Jewel of Russia (hard winter wheat and rye) / Russia

Kissui (rice) / Japan

Potocki (rye) / Poland

Reyka (blend of wheat and barley)

Stolichnaya (wheat and rye) / Russia

Van Gogh (blend of wheat, corn, and barley) / Netherlands

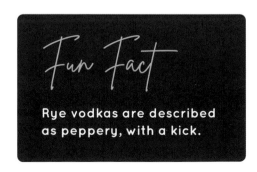

Fun Fact

Rye vodkas are described as peppery, with a kick.

Your Vodka, Your Way

Vodka enthusiasts are fanatical in their pursuit of life, liberty, and the purest vodka with the smoothest notes. Vodka is no longer to be dismissed as a tasteless, colorless, and odorless spirit to be splashed with cranberry juice in a dirty glass at a hole-in-the-wall bar.

These days, an ultra-smooth mouthful of ZYR vodka is at the top of my list. Once in a while, I'll mix up a batch of my husband's *current* favorite drink to have it waiting for him when he comes home from work. Sitting on the counter is a chilled tumbler of Florida CANE Blueberry Vodka and RumChata. *Mmmm-mmmm.* It legit tastes like a blueberry Creamsicle. And even though he's not usually a big fan of fruit or sweet drinks, my husband finds this vodka mix is the perfect way to unwind at the end of a busy day.

In our crazed world with maxed-out calendars, we need to stop and appreciate life's small pleasures. Instead of knocking back a few cold ones, we can find pleasure in a nice "sippable" vodka or mixed drink that melts away the stress. No matter how you take your vodka, it's time to savor the initial rush and mouthfeel. It's time to embrace the distinct flavors and unique notes. It's time to be a vodka snob.

Glassware

A well thought out drink recipe with quality vodka deserves a beautiful drinking vessel. Some drinks are recognizable by the glass they're poured into. Margaritas seem to taste best in sugar-rimmed fishbowls; martinis in sleek, thin-stemmed cones; mules in beautiful copper mugs; and mojitos in tall cylinders with a mint leaf garnish.

Truly, any glass will do, but please, for the love of snobbery everywhere, no red Solo® cups!

TYPES OF GLASSWARE

Here's a breakdown of the more common alcoholic beverage glassware types used to make the vodka drinks mentioned in this book:

- **Martini glass** (4–6 ounces): Thin-stemmed, *v*-shaped cocktail glass.

- **Lowball** (also known as an old-fashioned or rocks glass; 6–10 ounces): Short, heavy tumbler used for drinks on the rocks or with ice. There are also thicker rocks glasses that can be used to muddle (press fresh ingredients to release the flavors).

- **Highball glass** (6–10 ounces): Tall, narrow glasses used for doubles, Highballs, and fizzes.

- **Coupe** (7 ounces): Shaped like a wine glass but with a wider mouth; best for drinks served straight up (without ice).

- **Collins** (12–14 ounces): Named for the Collins cocktail, this glass is thinner than a highball.

- **Copper mug** (16 ounces): Often used for Moscow mules.

- **Shot glass** (2 ounces): The most recognizable alcoholic serving glass by far!

Other Equipment for Home Use

When entertaining one weekend, my husband and I tested out a Vodka Mojito recipe on our guests, only to realize we had never picked out a mortar and pestle during the day's shopping excursion. Instead of looking super suave as hosts, we crushed the mint with our fingers and ended up ripping it instead of muddling. We also forgot to add the sweetener so our poor friends' mojitos turned out to be a bitter-tasting flop.

Lesson learned. What we should have done as pestle-less hosts was place the chopped fresh mint leaves in a sealed sandwich bag and used a rolling pin to crush them, releasing their oils. To avoid your own hosting faux pas, here is a simple list of bar and mixing equipment to have on hand.

- **Cocktail shaker** Useful for thoroughly mixing and cooling cocktails.

- **Jigger** Used to measure ounces, a jigger is more accurate than a shot glass. Here's where things can get a little tricky: a jigger can also be used as a measurement equal to 1½ fluid ounces, although a large jigger will measure out 2 fluid ounces.

- **Citrus press** Being a true vodka snob means only using the best ingredients, like fresh-pressed citrus juices.

- **Zester** A fresh citrus twist is an elegant garnish for a vodka cocktail.

Terms of Measurements

- **Finger** Typically reserved for whisky, a finger refers to about an inch of liquid, or the amount if you were to pour the alcohol about the height of a finger wrapped around the glass.

- **Jigger** A piece of measuring equipment, but also a term of measurement equal to 1½ fluid ounces.

- **Pony** This term isn't used very often, but a pony is a shot equaling 1 fluid ounce.

- **Shots** Small servings of alcohol, roughly 1¼–1½ fluid ounce.

- **Tot** A half-shot.

Now that we've covered the basics, it's time to explore the classics. The drinks in the next chapter serve as the base for the most popular vodka drinks around. But before we get started, let's talk about a different kind of classic—the Tom Collins, which is traditionally a drink made with gin. A good tip for any vodka snob is that gin and vodka are usually interchangeable. So mix yourself up a Vodka Collins. You're going to love it!

Classic Vodka Collins

Ingredients

2 ounces vodka

½ ounce simple syrup

1 ounce lemon juice, freshly squeezed

Club soda, just a splash

Garnish maraschino cherry and orange peel or orange slice

Instructions

1. Pour all ingredients into a Collins glass.

2. Stir gently.

3. Garnish with an orange wedge (or peel) and a bright, beautiful maraschino cherry.

Grab your drink and let's get started!

CLASSIC VODKA COCKTAILS

t's time to talk about the classics! In his app *Modern Classics of the Cocktail Renaissance*, reviewed in an article by Jennifer Nalewicki for Tales of the Cocktail, drinks and bar reporter Robert Simonson shares three criteria that make a drink timeless:

- The drink needs to have traveled beyond the bar where it was invented.

- Customers need to know how to order it by name.

- The bartending community needs to hold the drink in high esteem.

Let's explore the world of classic cocktails, including martinis, Screwdrivers, Cape Codders, mules, and Black Russians, all of which easily pass the test for timeless beverages.

Martinis and Martini Lore

Look no further than the martini for the most classic of vodka drinks. While martinis are traditionally made from a combination of gin and vermouth, you can easily substitute vodka for gin in many cocktail recipes. Martinis can be made dry by using a dry vermouth, but many purists consider the perfect martini to be made with a one-to-one combination of sweet and dry vermouth.

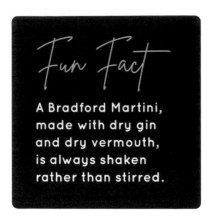

If you want to go straight for the iconic James Bond martini, you'll want a Vesper, which combines gin and vodka with Kina Lillet, a white wine liquor mixed with fruit and flavored with quinine. Sadly, Kina Lillet is no longer available—people lost their acquired taste for quinine when they left the colonies and found safer treatments for malaria. But if you're a hardcore 007 fan, you can add some quinine-infused liquor to Lillet Blanc, the sweeter and fruitier successor to Kina Lillet. Just know that the FDA has strong feelings about quinine, warning about its use in 1994, and banning almost all drugs with the ingredient in 2006.

With all the variations on the classic martini, you probably won't miss the Vesper, but you might have to drink a lot of martinis before you figure out exactly how you prefer your drink. Let's journey through some martini terms, so, like James Bond, you'll know how to answer the question, "How do you take your martini?" with savoir faire.

SHAKEN OR STIRRED?

Shaking a martini, aka James Bond's preference, helps the vermouth dissolve better and taste less oily. However, shaken martinis appear cloudier than stirred ones and get more diluted as the ice melts. Additionally, shaking can "bruise" the gin, which means it can become bitter. The benefits of a stirred martini are less dilution and a clearer drink with no ice chips from the shaking.

WET OR DRY?

When you order a martini wet or dry, you are indicating the amount of vermouth versus gin or vodka you prefer. A true vodka snob will know exactly how they enjoy this iconic cocktail and how to tailor it for their guests, so have fun taste-testing until you find your perfect martini!

- **Classic Martini** Recipes vary, but classic martinis are typically a combination of two and one-half parts gin or vodka to one-half part vermouth, although many recipes will increase the amount of gin or vodka.

- **Dry Martini** A dry martini has less vermouth than the classic martini. The gin (or vodka) to vermouth ratio should be five parts gin to one part vermouth (or higher). According to David Embury, author of *The Fine Art of Mixing Drinks*, the perfect ratio of five to one is the most pleasing to the average palate, although his personal preference is seven to one.

- **Wet Martini** Wet martinis have a higher percentage of vermouth, typically in a three-to-one ratio. SeriousEats.com contributor Niki Achitoff-Gray likes an equal combination of gin and vermouth with added olive brine, creating a more mellow and savory version.

- **Extra Wet Martini, aka Fifty-Fifty Martini** A one-to-one ratio of gin to vermouth.

- **Perfect Martini** Perfect martinis use a combination of 50 percent sweet vermouth and 50 percent dry vermouth.

DIRTY OR FILTHY?

Dirty and filthy martinis are flavored with brine and garnished with olives or caper-berries. A Gibson martini will come with pickled pearl onions, if that's your thing.

- **Dirty martini** A martini with added olive brine and an olive garnish

- **Filthy martini** A filthy martini replaces the olive brine with caperberry brine and takes a caperberry garnish.

NEAT, SERVED UP, OR ON THE ROCKS?

When ordering a drink, let the bartender know the temperature level you want your beverage.

- **Neat** Without ice.

- **Served Up** Chilled.

- **On the Rocks** With ice.

The Classic Vodka Martini, STIRRED

Using a high-quality vodka for a martini is crucial. I recommend Hangar 1 or Belvedere. For best results, chill your glass before mixing the martini.

Ingredients

2½ ounces vodka

½ ounce dry vermouth

Ice

Lemon peel twists or olives (stuffed or regular) for garnish

Instructions

1. Add vodka and dry vermouth to a mixing glass.
2. Add ice and stir until liquid is chilled.
3. Strain into cocktail glass.
4. Garnish with your choice of olives or lemon twist.

The Classic Vodka Martini, SHAKEN

Again, a high-quality vodka and chilled glass are essential for a great martini. For a beautiful vodka that won't break the bank, I recommend Belvedere or Hangar 1.

Ingredients

2½ ounces vodka

½ ounce dry vermouth

Ice as needed for shaker

Lemon peel twists or olives (stuffed or regular) for garnish

Instructions

1. Add vodka and dry vermouth to a cocktail shaker.
2. Add ice and shake for about ten seconds.
3. Strain through a fine-mesh strainer to remove any ice chips.
4. Pour into cocktail glass.
5. Garnish.

Blue Cheese–Stuffed Olives

Blue-cheese-stuffed olives are a decadent addition to a martini. Grab a jar from the supermarket or try this recipe adapted from Publix Aprons (http://www.publix.com /aprons-recipes/blue-cheese-stuffed-martini-olives), and make them at home.

Ingredients

40 pitted whole large green olives
⅓ cup blue cheese crumbles
2 ounces cream cheese, softened
2 teaspoons dry vermouth
Cayenne pepper
Slivered almonds for garnish

Instructions

1. Add blue cheese crumbles and cream cheese in medium bowl.
2. Beat with an electric mixer until creamy.
3. Stir in vermouth and cayenne pepper.
4. Spoon cheese mixture into pastry bag or quart-sized plastic bag with the tip cut off.
5. Pipe the cheese mixture into an olive.
6. Garnish with a slivered almond if serving as an appetizer; leave the almond out if using in a drink.
7. Serve olives immediately or place in an airtight container.
8. Cover and chill for up to 24 hours.
9. Let stand 10 minutes before serving.

Vodka and Fruit

Vodka and fruit are a great pairing. The Screwdriver and Cape Codder are both classic drinks in and of themselves, but they also act as great bases for countless variations. Let's take a look at the origins and recipes for several classic vodka-based drinks, so you can start sipping away.

Classic Screwdriver

The Screwdriver originated in the 1950s when oil-rig workers combined orange juice and vodka in cans and stirred them with their . . . you guessed it . . . screwdrivers. This well-loved drink may come from humble beginnings, but it remains a popular beverage that you can serve with pride.

Ingredients
2 ounces vodka

5 ounces orange juice

Ice

Slice of orange for garnish

Instructions
1. Combine vodka and orange juice in a chilled highball glass with ice.

2. Stir.

3. Garnish with orange slice. Actual screwdriver not required.

Fun Fact

Outside of the United States, the Screwdriver is known simply as "vodka and orange."

CONTROVERSIAL CRANBERRIES

I love stories of how things were invented, especially when the inspiration is due to a stroke of entrepreneurial genius. My favorite example is how the Michelin Tire Company came up with restaurant ratings to get their customers to drive farther out of town, thus wearing out their tires faster. Now Michelin stars are prestigious awards and highly revered by chefs globally. Tires. Food. Brilliant!

Similarly, the Cape Codder, aka "vodka and cran," was developed to promote sales as well. This classic is named for its origins in Cape Cod, Massachusetts; however, the drink was originally called the Red Devil and invented by none other than the Ocean Spray cranberry growers' cooperative. In fact, it was due to these growers' efforts to make cranberry juice a common "drink mixer" that many of these vodka and cranberry variations exist.

Here's what happened. The U.S. Secretary of Health warned Americans to avoid cranberries when some were found to contain traces of an herbicide linked with cancer. This left cranberry growers with a lot of berries and not a lot of customers. Ocean Spray began marketing cocktails that included cranberry juice, and the rest, as they say, is tart and delicious history.

Classic Cape Codder, aka Vodka Cranberry

The classic vodka-to-cran ratio is one part vodka to two parts cranberry juice. Enjoy!

Ingredients
2 ounces vodka
4 ounces cranberry juice
Ice
Lime wedge for garnish

Instructions
1. Fill a glass with ice (we recommend a highball).
2. Pour the cranberry juice and vodka over the ice.
3. Stir.
4. Garnish with a lime wedge, and feel free to squeeze some of that fresh lime juice into the glass.

Classic Greyhound

The Greyhound is a close cousin to the Cape Codder, substituting grapefruit juice for cranberry juice. The classic ratio is one part vodka to two parts grapefruit juice.

Ingredients

2 ounces vodka

4 ounces grapefruit juice

Ice

Lime wedge for garnish

Instructions

1. Fill a glass with ice (we recommend a highball).

2. Pour the grapefruit juice and vodka over the ice.

3. Stir.

4. Garnish with lime wedge, and feel free to squeeze some of that fresh lime juice into the glass.

Note Dampen the rim of your glass and dip it in salt before mixing, and you've turned this Greyhound into a Salty Dog.

Classic Sea Breeze Cocktail

One of the more popular drinks in the 1970s was the Sea Breeze cocktail, which is a combination of the Cape Codder and Greyhound. This delicious drink started out as a gin and hibiscus grenadine concoction in the 1920s and then segued into apricot brandy and lemon juice post-Prohibition. Today, the Sea Breeze recipe is one part vodka, two parts cranberry juice, and one part grapefruit juice.

Ingredients

2 ounces vodka

4 ounces cranberry juice

2 ounces grapefruit juice

Ice

Lime wedge for garnish

Instructions

1. Fill a glass with ice (we recommend a highball).

2. Pour the cranberry juice, pineapple juice, and vodka over the ice.

3. Stir.

4. Garnish with lime wedge, and feel free to squeeze some of that fresh lime juice into the glass.

Classic Bay Breeze Cocktail

The Bay Breeze Cocktail is yet another riff off the Cape Codder, with sweet pineapple juice added to the cranberry and vodka original. The classic ratio for a Bay Breeze is one part vodka, two parts cranberry juice, and one part pineapple juice.

Ingredients

2 ounces vodka

4 ounces cranberry juice

2 ounces pineapple juice

Ice

Lime wedge for garnish

Instructions

1. Fill a glass with ice (we recommend a highball).
2. Pour the cranberry juice, pineapple juice, and vodka over the ice.
3. Stir.
4. Garnish with lime wedge, and feel free to squeeze some of that fresh lime juice into the glass.

Rose Kennedy Cocktail

The Rose Kennedy Cocktail is named after the mother of the late president John F. Kennedy. If you garnish a Rose Kennedy with a lime instead of a lemon, the name of this drink changes to an Ethel Kennedy, named after Bobby Kennedy's wife.

When ordering this drink at bars, the Rose Kennedy is typically referred to as a "vodka soda, splash of cran."

Ingredients

2 ounces vodka

2 ounces club soda

Splash of cranberry juice

Ice

Lemon wedge for garnish

Instructions

1. Fill a rocks glass with ice.
2. Pour the club soda and vodka over ice.
3. Add a splash of cranberry to your preferred pink color.
4. Stir.
5. Garnish with lemon wedge or lime wedge, depending on which of the Kennedys you prefer.

Madras Cocktail

Our final variation on the Cape Codder is the Madras, which is full of citrus brilliance. The classic Madras cocktail is one shot of vodka deliciously mixed with cranberry juice and orange juice.

Ingredients

1½ ounces vodka
1 ounce orange juice
4 ounces cranberry juice
Ice
Lime wedge for garnish

Instructions

1. Fill a highball glass with ice.
2. Add vodka, cranberry juice, and orange juice.
3. Stir.
4. Garnish with a lime wedge.

MORE THAN A PINK DRINK

The Cosmopolitan had a resurgence in popularity thanks to HBO's *Sex and the City*, but this blush-colored beverage didn't get its start as a pink girly drink. Former Odeon nightclub bartender Toby Cecchini told Cait Munro for *Refinery 29* he invented the Cosmo after making a San Francisco cocktail he had heard about that consisted of Rose's lime and grenadine. He hated it. But he liked the pink color, so Cecchini remade the cocktail using fresh lime juice, Cointreau, citrus vodka, cranberry juice, and a twist of lemon.

The Cosmopolitan quickly became an Odeon staff favorite and then a widespread hit, and even though Cecchini's recipe isn't the one that's followed for the majority of Cosmos today, we tip our hat to him for the inspired recipe and to *Sex and the City* for the glamour they brought to this delicious drink.

The Classic Cosmopolitan

Ingredients

1½ ounces vodka

¼ ounce lime juice

¼ ounce cranberry juice

¼ ounce triple sec

1 cup ice

Lime wedge (or lemon twist)
for garnish

Instructions

1. Add lime juice, triple sec,
   vodka, cranberry juice,
   and ice to a cocktail shaker.

2. Shake well.

3. Strain into cocktail glass and
   serve with a lime wedge . . .
   or pay tribute to Cecchini
   with a lemon twist garnish.

Sex on the Beach

Move over *Sex and the City*—it's time for Sex on the Beach. The folklore surrounding the cocktail's name dates back to 1987 when "Ted the bartender" created a cocktail to sell the newest rage: peach schnapps. According to legend, Ted named the drink Sex on the Beach after spring breakers' two favorite things.

The one caveat to this tale, according to Julie R. Thomson for the *Huffington Post*, is that in 1982, just five short years before "Ted" named the cocktail, bartenders had already invented the Sex on the Beach, likely by combining a Fuzzy Navel with a Cape Codder.

Whichever story you choose to believe, Sex on the Beach is a fruity blend of awesome. If you can't bring yourself to order it out loud at a bar, you can easily make it at home.

Ingredients
1½ ounces vodka
1½ ounces orange juice
1½ ounces cranberry juice
¾ ounce peach schnapps
1 cup ice
Orange slice for garnish

Instructions
1. Add all the ingredients to a highball glass.
2. Garnish with an orange slice.

Bloody Mary

The Bloody Mary deserves its own category because even though the tomato is *technically* a fruit, this classic brunch go-to is in a class of its own.

My first Bloody Mary experience was at a little eatery on the main road of our town. The Bloody Mary was served in a Collins glass, filled almost to the rim with a beautiful, rusty-colored concoction full of spices. The classic celery stalk was lush, green, and vibrant. I was nervous that it would taste like a glass of V-8 mixed with vodka, but thankfully I was mistaken. That first sip filled my palate with richness and spice, and I instantly fell in love.

What's great about the Bloody Mary is that it can be customized to virtually any palate, but to make a truly delicious version, one must respect the balance of ingredients. The inevitable spice and kick from the tomato-based beverage comes with a significant amount of sodium, which, if out of balance, can make the drink taste too salty.

NAME ORIGINS

There is a bit of controversy over who actually invented the Bloody Mary: bartender Fernand Petiot in 1920 or actor/comedian George Jessel in the 1930s.

There seem to be lines drawn in that dispute, although Petiot is quoted in a 1964 *New Yorker* article saying that Jessel started the drink on its way with a combination of vodka and tomato juice, but that he finished it by adding the spices, lemon, and Worcestershire. Either way, we're just glad that the Bloody Mary exists in its spicy, savory fashion.

Additionally, there is debate over why the Bloody Mary is named "Bloody Mary." Many believe the drink is named after Queen Mary I of England, but

Wisconsin is home to a delightful Bloody Mary tradition: a sidecar of beer accompanying every Bloody Mary order. Why a beer chaser? Truthfully, no one really knows, but all agree the presentation is phenomenal.

there are some who hold to the drink being named after a waitress or actress Mary Pickford.

THE MORE GARISH THE GARNISH . . .

As far as garnish goes, there doesn't seem to be a *wrong* way to garnish a Bloody Mary, but we prefer garnishes of the elegant variety. The classic celery stick, olives, pickles, and even pickled green beans are typical accoutrements, although in some parts of the United States, you may find string cheese, shrimp, or, according to *Thrillist*'s food and drink writer Kristin Hunt, even a whole fried chicken.

According to Brian Bartels, author of *The Bloody Mary,* the drink should never be shaken. Instead, he recommends the method called *rolling,* which entails the drink being carefully poured between two shakers. This gentler method prevents an unpleasant tomato foam forming on the top of your drink.

Hunt says the "Chicken Fried Bloody Mary" debuted in 2014 at Milwaukee's Sobelman's Bar and Grill at a price tag of $50. Included with the whole chicken were garnishes of bacon-wrapped jalapeño cheeseball skewers, shrimp, sausage, and in case you weren't getting enough veggies, Brussels sprouts, mushrooms, scallions, onion, and asparagus.

If you're ready to make your own take on this classic, use this recipe as a base. And really, the sky's the limit.

Basic Bloody Mary

Ingredients

2 ounces vodka

4 ounces tomato juice

½ ounce fresh lemon juice

2 teaspoons prepared horseradish

2 dashes of Worcestershire sauce

2 dashes of Tabasco sauce

1 pinch each of celery salt, ground black pepper, and smoked paprika

Lemon or lime wedge, celery stalk, green olives, or rimming spices for garnish (whole fried chicken optional)

Instructions

1. Combine ingredients in a cocktail shaker or tall glass.

2. Roll the drink by pouring it back and forth between the two glasses. If you have to shake instead of rolling, shake very gently.

3. Strain over and onto fresh ice in a cocktail glass.

4. Garnish with a lemon wedge and celery stalk and enjoy!

Note For an extra special look, rim the glass with salt or a specialty spice mix.

Mules

The Moscow Mule is seriously one of my favorite drinks. The basic composition of a mule is ginger beer and citrus. For the Moscow Mule, the liquor of choice is vodka. For the Kentucky Mule, it's bourbon.

Ginger beer is refreshing and soothing with a little spicy warm kick toward the end. Plus, who doesn't adore those pretty copper mugs they come in? Oprah, who also favors the Moscow Mule, adds a sprig of fresh mint as garnish.

The history behind this iconic drink is a fascinating tale of entrepreneurial spirit and gumption, despite the various renditions of how it came to be.

Story 1 According to most accounts, all of which seem to be posted on GoMoscowMule.com, there were three inventors of the mule: businessman John Martin (who'd just acquired Smirnoff), Cock 'n' Bull bar owner Jack Morgan (who was struggling to sell his ginger beer), and a third party who was either Morgan's girlfriend, Smirnoff's former owner and then executive Rudolph Kunett, or some other person who had a large stash of copper mugs they wanted to move. Natasha Frost of *Gastro Obscura* identifies the third inventor as Morgan's girlfriend and an heiress to a struggling copper factory.

Story 2 According to Eric Felton in the *Wall Street Journal*, head Cock 'n' Bull bartender Will Price invented the Moscow Mule when he mixed the overstock of Martin's Smirnoff vodka and Morgan's ginger beer.

Story 3 In yet a third story, told by MoscowCopper.com, Russian emigrant Sophia Berezinski traveled to America with two thousand copper mugs of her own design from her father's copper factory. On her husband's insistence to sell the mugs or have them tossed into the trash heap, Sophia went door-to-door looking for a buyer. One providential day, she entered the Cock 'n' Bull bar where John Martin and Jack Morgan were meeting to discuss their individual hardships. The three of them each brought a piece of the Moscow Mule puzzle: vodka, ginger beer, and the iconic copper mugs.

My personal favorite of the three stories includes Sophie's contribution, but no matter which origin story is true, the Moscow Mule continues to be a classic favorite, as well as a drink that I love to make when I have guests drop by, particularly on a hot summer day.

Moscow Mule

Ingredients

2 ounces vodka

½ ounce fresh lime juice

6 ounces ginger beer (*not* ginger ale)

Ice

Lime wedge for garnish (or follow Oprah's example and add mint)

Instructions

1. Add lime juice and ice to either a copper Moscow Mule mug or a Collins glass.

2. Combine the vodka and ginger beer (again, *not* ginger ale) over ice and stir.

3. Garnish with lime wedge. Enjoy!

Vodka and Coffee

Black Russian & White Russian

The Black Russian made its debut in 1949, and the White Russian quickly followed suit when drinkers added cream to the mix.

Ingredients
2 ounces vodka

1 ounce coffee liqueur

Ice (as desired)

For a White Russian, add a splash of cream.

Instructions
1. Mix ingredients in a lowball or rocks glass and stir.

Mudslide

The origins of the Mudslide go back to the 1950s at the Wreck Bar in the Cayman Islands. Known as the adult milkshake, the Mudslide boasts vodka, ice cream, Kahlua, and Bailey's. To elevate this drink, use a high-quality vodka, a premium ice cream, and, if you're feeling particularly snobby, add in some crème de cacao.

Ingredients

1½ ounces vodka

1½ ounces Irish cream

1½ ounces Kahlua

4–8 ounces ice cream (vanilla or chocolate, it's up to you!)

Optional 1 ounce crème de cacao

Add chocolate syrups, sprinkles, cherries, or whatever floats your boat for garnish

Instructions

1. In a blender, combine vodka, Irish cream, Kahlua, ice cream, and crème de cacao (if you're using it).

2. Cover and blend.

3. Pour into frosty fun glasses and add garnish. Enjoy!

HOW TO ORDER

didn't drink until I was twenty-one. On our honeymoon, my husband introduced me to several mixed-drink concoctions, and my taste buds experienced
a whirlwind of flavor profiles. Having never purchased alcohol before, I was
intrigued by the lingo my husband used to order the drinks. It was like asking
for an elixir from a magician while at the same time telling them exactly how to
prepare it. I was insecure, to say the least, about using the wrong verbiage or ordering something I didn't like. Luckily my husband was fluent in "bar-speak" and a
willing tutor. Here are some tips to help you enjoy your cocktails and feel confident
with cocktail culture.

Who Takes the Drink Order?

Many restaurants allow the waitstaff to take drink orders, while others require
you to order alcohol directly from the bartender. Some venues require you to sit
in the bar area as opposed to drinking at your table. I made a few mistakes when
ordering drinks, so here are some of the tips I've learned.

If you're ordering your drinks from a waiter or waitress, feel free to ask
questions about the drinks the same way you would discuss chef specials or food
menu items. Be considerate of their time, but make sure they understand your
order, because they are more than likely going to have to transcribe that drink
request to the bartender for its preparation.

If you're ordering at the bar, you should also feel welcome to ask questions,
but as with the waitstaff, it's important to respect the bartender's time. The

more drinks a bartender can serve up within a limited amount of time the more revenue they will generate for their establishment and the more tips they will garner for themselves. A good bartender will make you feel like they have all the time in the world to dialogue with you about your drink selection, but the opposite is closer to the truth—time is money. Bartenders make the majority of their wages from tips, so knowing how and what to order will keep you from entering into their bad graces.

Standing and Walk-Up Bar Etiquette

Understanding the unspoken etiquette about sitting at a bar—or standing at a walk-up bar—will earn you top service and the appreciation of the staff and other customers.

Rule number one Stay out of the area where the waitstaff pick up drinks for the dining room guests. This is usually a sectioned-off area with brass or other style rails. As my husband says, if you are in this area, you are in the way. *I'm sorry to say that I've often been in the way, so I've heard this more than once!*

Rule number two You don't have to be sitting or standing at the bar to place a drink order. Bars have a limited number of seats, and so many people feel like they need to wait until a seat is available in order to request drink service. But if you can't make it to the bar, simply make eye contact with the bartender and wait your turn. If you can't get their attention, raising your hand slightly—like an older southern gentleman bidding at auction—should do the trick. The goal here is to briefly draw the attention of the bar staff.

Once your patience is rewarded, it's time to order. Bartenders are generally busy so be sure to speak clearly and keep it short, but there are a few things to consider before making your final selection.

"Do You Have Any Drink Specials?"

This is a question that's always worth asking. When I inquire about drink specials, I often receive a rundown of their beer specials, which is *not* what I'm after. It's okay to specifically ask for *liquor* drink specials. This saves the bartender or waitstaff time and allows you to focus only on what you really want to hear.

Know Your Alcohol Classifications

There are three main classifications of alcohols: well, call, and top shelf. Let's dive in!

WELL BRANDS

Well drinks (aka wells) are generally less recognizable brands typically located directly behind the bar for easy access. They are significantly cheaper for the bar to purchase and are the standard liquor added to an inexpensive mixed drink, although some places will have "Premium Well" brands, which is a great thing for the consumer! Using well brands is a great way for bars to increase profit and provide good value for the less discerning drinker.

When you specify the type of alcohol or cocktail only and not the name brand—"rum and coke," "vodka and cran," or "Long Island Iced Tea"—you're ordering well liquor. The beauty of these well brands is their affordability, and if you are going to mix the liquor with a strong flavor, you will often lose the subtle flavors of the liquor itself anyway. For instance, you probably wouldn't spend the money to mix a premium Belvedere vodka with orange juice or Red Bull.

Quality matters, though, and the quality of well drinks is not always up to par. I once had a hotel well vodka with cranberry and after one sip I couldn't bring myself to finish it. I felt bad about wasting it but after upping my vodka game, I could taste the difference between the well vodka and the brands we were purchasing at home.

My husband enjoys a stiff drink every once in a while, but not every bar accommodates all the varieties of liquor. If you are ordering a bourbon, let's say, the bar's well may only have a generic whiskey to serve. Well whiskey may have caramel color added to improve its look, but this will not improve its flavor.

If you order something with well tequila, it will more often than not contain a concoction of grain alcohol with just a hint of the specialized agave liquor. The good news is that when you order well vodka you will get vodka, even though it may not be as filtered or have as pleasing a flavor profile. If a drink is going to be ordered up from the well, vodka is the wisest of moves.

Keep in mind that ordering anything from the well is not exactly being a vodka snob. If you can afford to treat yourself, order call or top-shelf drinks. They will generally taste better and leave you feeling better afterward. And there is something nice about ordering a favorite or new brand of vodka by name.

CALL BRANDS

Vodka aficionados, let's raise our ordering standards to the call drink, which is a mixed drink where the alcohol is mentioned by brand name. Think "Jack and Coke," or "Stoli and cranberry." Most bars have a fancy mirrored display full of name-brand liquors. Compared to well liquor, the name-brand bottles are exquisite and the brands recognizable. These are the bottles the bar is proud to display.

Many bars organize their alcohol by type of liquor in a left-to-right manner. While this isn't a hard-and-fast rule, generally one side has dark liquors like rum, bourbon, or whisky, and the other side will have clear liquors like gin or vodka.

These call drinks are where you should set your vodka-snob minimum standard. Call drinks are a bit pricier than the cheaper well versions, but sometimes it's better to consume a couple of quality drinks versus several from the well. The age old saying holds true for beverages: choose quality over quantity.

TOP-SHELF BRANDS

Premium liquors are often featured in elevated locations overlooking the other brands within their domain. These top-shelf varieties are considered to be the "best of the best" and have the price tags to prove it. Top-shelf bottles do not need to be placed within easy reach for the bartender, since the majority of drinks are made from the well or call shelves. Their lofty locations confer a level of prestige, both for the brand and the consumer. When you order top shelf, you are treating yourself to a higher standard. You are becoming a customer who values the nuances that producers of top-shelf vodkas spend the time, energy, and resources to get just right.

Even for this self-proclaimed vodka snob, my palate is not developed enough to appreciate the subtle nuances of a top-shelf vodka when it's mixed with juice or soda. And many times, the price difference between ordering a top-shelf vodka over a "call brand" means it will be a one-drink-only kind of night. However, there are benefits to ordering top shelf at a bar, such as providing an opportunity to taste premium brands before dropping the cash for a full bottle. I'd much rather spend eight or nine dollars on a drink to decide if I like the brand and flavor combination before spending money on a full bottle of vodka that I won't enjoy.

Stay true to your taste preferences, but don't spend money unnecessarily for pure pretentiousness.

ALL ABOUT FLAVOR
AND FLAVOR FANATICS

Vodka. **To flavor** or not to flavor?
I believe the answer to that question is all about personal preference. As we refine our palates and choose higher quality brands of vodka, it becomes more tempting to sip it without any type of additive.

Despite the popularity of flavored vodkas, often used in cocktails, many traditionalists shy away. In a 2008 *New York Times* article, author and cocktail expert David Wondrich is quoted as sarcastically saying "Why squeeze lemon juice when you can pour in some lemon vodka?"

I have so much respect for the expert mixologists and love to learn from their experience and knowledge. However, since my palette has not elevated to the point where I prefer my vodka straight (and I believe the majority of us newly inducted vodka snobs would agree), we're going to jump into this world of flavor and see where it takes us.

When done right, flavored vodkas add depth. Cîroc's berry flavored vodka is a beautiful addition to a cola, replacing the need for grenadine and saving a ton of calories. Florida Cane's Key West Lemon and Lime is our go-to for Moscow Mules.

But beyond the addition of flavorings, there are other considerations to take into account that affect the flavor profile of your preferred type of vodka, including the base product used (wheat, grape, potato, and so on), the number of times the vodka is distilled and filtered, and what the vodka is filtered through. Let's jump in!

The Distillery Difference

While many consider vodka to be tasteless, the distillation process has a profound effect on flavor. Many brands go through several rounds of distillation and filtering to maximize the flavor profile. As the vodka market grows, there is increased attention to quality and demand for distinction. These days even neutral vodkas contain subtle flavor notes.

If you are a vodka newbie, a great way to learn about the varieties of vodka flavors is through distillery tours, which typically include tastings. Middle West Spirits, a craft distillery in Columbus, Ohio, is one example of a venue that passes out samples of vodkas, rums, and whiskeys, and there is likely a similar tour near you.

Fun Fact

According to VodkaFacts.com's "History of Vodka," we can thank the inventors of distillation not only for fine liquors and vodkas but also for the modern perfume industry. The first use of distilleries in ancient days was to create much-needed aromatics for personal hygiene, not stronger alcohol.

Filtering

The goal of filtration is to remove the smallest amounts of impurities and to smooth out the flavor. There are a variety of ingredients or components that vodka can be distilled from (mash), as well as a variety of filters that can be used in the distillation process. Some distillers will even forego filtration all together.

The most common brands of vodkas are distilled from wheat or potatoes, however, and are filtered, at least once, through standard, wood-based charcoal.

A company's filtration process can also be used as a marketing ploy or sales gimmick, like brands who filter their vodka through diamonds.

Yes, *diamonds*.

Some brands may even go so far as to adorn their bottles with gold embellishments and, yes, more diamonds. Sadly, I'm not in a position to sample these multimillion-dollar bottles of vodka, and I think it's safe to assume that many of us aren't.

Ultimately, though, taste is what matters, and here we enter the beautiful world of craft distilleries, where small batches of vodka are created with close attention to quality and unique flavor profiles. For the non–diamond filtered vodka lovers amongst us, let's keep our sights set on these attainable—and still delicious—vodkas.

Cindy Augustine for Liquor.com lists many factors that affect the taste and all-important mouth feel of vodka, starting with the mash, the water qualities, the pumps, the aging, the type of still, and the filtration method. For sippers of fine vodkas, Augustine says, filtration is a big one. Because filtration removes impurities, it will also remove flavor and texture: those who sip vodka neat will need to decide if they like a pure, thin, super-filtered vodka, or a thicker, creamier, less filtered vodka with a more robust flavor. The number of filtration steps matters—from multiple filtrations to none—but the *type* of filter may also matter to you. Whether you are attracted to the prestige of diamond filtration or the ecological advantages of sustainable filtering materials, here are some filtration basics to get you started.

TYPES OF FILTERING SYSTEMS

There's a lot of diversity in filtration processes, but these three types of filtering systems are going to account for most of the vodkas you'll find on the shelves of your local liquor stores:

Charcoal filtering The majority of vodka producers use some form of charcoal filtering, mostly wood charcoal, but substances ranging from lava rocks to coconut husks can also be used.

Micron filtering Several vodka distillers utilize a micron paper filter to remove any additional impurities that may have hung around during the distillation process.

No Filtering Some distillers feel that their unique combination of water and distillation produces the ideal product and prefer not to do filtering of any kind.

Filtering your vodka is just one of the steps that master craftsmen will go through in order to round out their top-quality product. Quality vodka is crafted from the ground up and not just compiled at the very end. Here are a few notable vodkas, however, that set themselves apart with their unique twist on these basic filtering methods.

Bamboo Charcoal

Haku vodka, from Japan, is distilled by the House of Suntory from the best 100 percent Japanese white rice and filtered through bamboo charcoal. According to HakuVodka.Suntory.com, the name *Haku* means "white" or "brilliant," making it the ideal name for their vodka, which they describe as "luminous." The House of Suntory was founded in 1899 by a young man named Shinjiro Torii, who wanted to make a spirit that distilled the elemental qualities of Japanese nature and craftmanship. Haku Vodka prides themselves on using sustainable ingredients and fast-growing, low–environmental impact bamboo for its filtration charcoal. They claim that bamboo charcoal is more porous than traditional wood charcoal and that the minerals in the charcoal leave the finished vodka with a clean, sweet taste and smooth, mellow finish.

You may be unable to get to Japan to tour Haku's distillery in person, but the chances are great that you can interact with them during a local tasting event, or, as is now common, you could visit them online.

Wood and Coconut Husks

Florida Cane vodka, a personal favorite of my husband's, is distilled from sugar cane and then drip filtered through a unique charcoal comprised of coconut husks, which leaves behind a unique flavor, according to Breanne Williams of the *Plant City Observer*. Williams calls Florida Cane vodka an "entirely American product. The bottles come from Missouri, the corks from outside of Michigan and everything inside the bottle is 100 percent Floridian." If you're able to get to Ybor City, Florida Cane Distilleries has plant tours, liquor tastings, bartending classes, and even a make-your-own-whiskey course where you take your own bottle home to age.

Lava Rock

Reyka brand vodka is from Iceland, the land of volcanoes. According to their website, Reyka.com, Reyka uses arctic spring water from melted glaciers in their unique distillation process, warms their plant with geothermal heat, and filters their finished product through the lava rocks that they have in abundance. It is another brand that locally sources their products, and another uniquely local way to filter vodka.

Diamonds

Crystal Head Vodka takes charcoal filtering to the next level and uses diamonds for three of the seven filtration passes on their Aurora labeled vodka. Technically, according to their web page for the label, they use Herkimer diamonds which are actually a partially rare quartz crystal, but they still look really cool and achieve the type of amazing smoothness that all vodka snobs are searching for.

No Filter

The Belvedere brand positions themselves as the first super-premium vodka, and in keeping with that refined position they have released an unfiltered vodka that has left its mark among top-tier liquors. Belvedere Unfiltered is distilled from rye and bottled without filtration to ensure the flavoring essence is intact. Chip

Dykstra of the *Rum Howler Blog* describes that essence as having freshly baked bread or milk chocolate notes. Because of this distinct nose and flavor some have labeled Belvedere Unfiltered a whiskey drinker's vodka.

Every distillery has their own flavor palate, which is the result of extensive tasting and experimentation. Distilling from corn will produce a sweeter vodka, so filtering it through standard wood charcoal may produce the intended result. Alternatively distilling from sugar cane and filtering through wood charcoal will produce a palatable vodka, but it may not be what the distillers envisioned. Distillers try many distillate and filtration combinations until they achieve the vodka they approve of. The artful process of distilling and filtering (or not) is completely up to the producer's vision for their product. Each consumer comes with their distinct palate and preferred flavor profiles as well. Sample, taste, and sip as many brands as you can until you arrive at several that you like.

MIXED DRINKS

While vodka should taste great by itself, it can be elevated by mixing it with other spirits or juices. My friends, this is where vodka gets fun, but we can thank hard times for our wide variety of cocktails we enjoy today.

In an eye-opening history of Prohibition Era alcohol consumption for *Quartz*, Jeffrey Miller says that distilled spirits made up less than 40 percent of total alcohol consumption in America prior to prohibition but after "the noble experiment," accounted for 75 percent. Mixed drinks became popular as speakeasies and partygoers mixed in beverages and additives to mask the flavor of rotgut liquor made from industrial alcohol or fly-by-night moonshiners.

Financial hardships for consumers and distillers throughout the Great Depression and World War II created a continuing need for blended drinks. Promoting cocktails was a financially sound business move in lean times: you could stretch limited liquor supplies and sell a single drink for less money since it had less alcohol.

For women or men interested in the world of bourbon, check out *How to Be a Bourbon Badass* (Red Lightning Books) to learn how to celebrate all things liquid gold.

In order to sell a nation on the idea of a "diluted drink," which since Prohibition had been associated with bootleggers and their questionable liquor, the fixers of the advertising game became essential in an era of new prosperity following World War II, as Reid Mitenbuler tells us in "What Are They Drinking on Mad Men?," a Drinking in History column for *Serious Eats*. Mixed liquors were rebranded as light, mild, smooth, and mellow, and mixed drinks became favorites in the female market. Even though women had always been alcohol consumers, some beverages were still considered a man's drink, such as bourbons, whiskeys, and beers.

We see this gendered drinking dichotomy in the hit series *Mad Men*. Set in the 1950s, the show follows advertising executives, particularly those working with the main character Don Draper. His secretary, Peggy Olson, eager to make a name for herself in this good ol' boys club, dips her fingers into whiskey, while Draper's wife, Betty, sticks to fruitier beverages like vodka gimlets that hide that breathier edge of alcohol.

Spotlight on Cirrus

Made primarily with Virginia russet potatoes, Cirrus vodka is triple-distilled, barely filtered, and cut to 80-proof with high-quality spring water. Water quality matters and the people at Cirrus ensure theirs is top notch.

According to an "abridged, inebriated history" of the Gimlet by the Gin Foundry, the drink dates back to the nineteenth century when British officers downed citrus juice to avoid catching scurvy. Some trace the drink back to Rear-Admiral Sir Thomas Desmond Gimlette, who doctored the lime juice with gin as a way to help the sailors swallow their medicine. Sailors also used rum to improve the taste of lime and called it grog. Others claim the Gimlet is named after the hand tool that is used to bore into the barrels on the Navy ships. Either way, it's a fun word to say and a fun drink to . . . well, drink.

Gimlet

In the 1950s novel *The Long Goodbye*, Raymond Chandler describes the gimlet as "half gin and half Rose's lime juice and nothing else." We're detouring from Chandler's recipe by substituting vodka for gin.

Ingredients
Sweetened lime juice (sailors of old turned to Rose's Lime Juice Cordial)

Vodka

Lime for garnish

Instructions
1. Mix two parts lime juice to two parts vodka.
2. Shake and serve.

Want to Make Your Own Lime Cordial?

Missing the fresh citrus taste in your gimlets or wanting to forego the high-fructose corn syrup in some bottled lime juices? Award-winning bartender and best-selling author Jeffrey Morgenthaler's recipe for lime cordial is simple, quick, and only involves 1 cup of sugar, 1.5 ounces of fresh-squeezed lime juice, 1.5 ounces grated lime peel (waste not, want not!), and 1 ounce of citric acid, all blended with 8 ounces of hot water (detailed instructions at JeffreyMorgenthaler.com). If you don't have citric acid, try using Crystal Light in various increments to taste. Cutting carbs or reducing sugar intake? Substitute Swerve (erythritol) which has a cooling effect, Stevia, or your favorite sugar replacement to taste.

Flavoring

There's a beautiful simplicity to a vodka soda with sliced lime, but flavored vodkas can kick your cocktail into high gear. Hate pulp or pieces of fruit in your drink? Instead of plain vodka, utilize some Stoli Lime to maintain the elegance of your drink.

Like any aspect of distilling vodka, each brand crafts their product with their own internal standards and acceptable outcomes. One method to flavor vodka is to add chemicals, juices, syrups, or extracts, similar to flavoring methods for sodas and waters. While flavored waters make us feel good for drinking water, flavoring in our vodka may leave us feeling less enthusiastic.

Not all vodkas are crafted equally, however, and the same rule applies for flavored vodkas. As a general rule, always check labels to see if the vodka is flavored with syrups, artificial ingredients, or sugars.

CREATIVE FLAVOR PROFILES

Flavored vodka is continually increasing in popularity, especially in the market of mixed liquors and cocktails. Flavorists in the vodka market today are brilliantly creative, adding essences of everything from honeysuckle to teas. The brand Van Gogh has combined the flavors of raspberries and peanuts, creating a trip down memory lane to peanut butter and jelly sandwiches. But when it comes to flavored vodkas, Pinnacle leads the pack with dessert flavors like Chocolate Whipped, which is a delicious addition to your late-night coffee. If you want to take your dessert-making to the next level, use Pinnacle's Le Double Espresso in your tiramisu.

Fun Fact

Chilling vodka can actually mute its imperfections. Sip vodkas at room temperature to get a true sampling.

EXTRACTS

Some of the best flavored vodkas are infused with real fruit juice extracts. Natural extracts provide a deeper level of flavor that lingers on the front of the tongue while the alcohol coats the back of the tongue and throat. Vodkas made using this method are typically labeled as containing all-natural flavors. They provide an overall sensational mouth experience and really enhance the flavor and sophistication of your beverages. Varieties of citrus tend to be the most common flavorings for vodka. This is most likely due to the beautiful marriage of citrus acidity and alcohol. Screwdriver, anyone?

INFUSIONS

Infusing flavor into vodka is an artisanal and time-consuming process, but it creates outstanding flavored vodkas. Flavor notes are more muted when compared to syrup- or extract-based alternatives, but the finished products have a significantly smoother and better taste. Quality-minded craft vodka brands typically infuse their alcohol with traditional source fruits such as oranges, limes, and strawberries, but according to Anna Archibald at *Thrillist*, pears, apples, blueberries, cucumbers, ginger, herbs, spices, peppers, and even

horseradish also lead to excellent results. And yes, there are chocolate and coffee infused vodkas, and they are delicious.

The infusion process is more time consuming than simply adding a few drops of flavoring to the mix. Some manufacturers may even leave rinds or pieces of fruits in their bottles to produce a richer flavor. Many distilleries that use this method re-distill the liquor in order to remove any residual fruit or flavoring material. Here are a few recipes that highlight naturally infused vodkas.

Blueberry Muffin Chata

Substitute this sweet concoction for your dessert. You won't be sorry.

Ingredients
Two (or equal) parts each:
    Blueberry vodka
    RumChata

Instructions
1. Mix RumChata and blueberry vodka
2. Shake and serve (over ice is optional).

Orange Crush

Ingredients
One part orange vodka
Two parts club soda
Ice as needed
Orange wedges

Instructions
1. Pour one part orange vodka to two parts club soda over ice.
2. Squeeze orange wedge over glass, then add wedge to glass.

(This recipe was adapted from KetelOne.com's Oranje Soda.)

Homemade DIY Skittles Vodka

Some popular artificially flavored vodkas come from the chewy, fruit-flavored confections that we grew up asking our parents for in the checkout aisle. Ahhh . . . nostalgia.

For instance, for those of us who love to "taste the rainbow," homemade Skittles vodka brings back that taste of childhood. The process involves separating the Skittles flavors into different containers, covering them with the vodka of your choice, and waiting for that fruity flavor to infiltrate the vodka. The cocktail masters at MixThatDrink.com suggest using empty water bottles, coffee filters and cheese cloths to strain out all the Skittles bits, and a mid-range vodka. Check out their step-by-step process with photos at MixThatDrink.com/Skittles-Vodka-Tutorial.

VODKA AND HOLLYWOOD

Cocktails and Hollywood go hand in hand like a childlike spirit and a Van Gogh PB&J Vodka cocktail, which, of course, we have a recipe for in a later chapter! Perception is everything, and a character's outfit speaks volumes for their social standing. If an actress's character sports a chic black cocktail dress with pearls, she is likely to be regarded as classy and timeless. The technology that an on-screen persona uses also provides insights to the audience. If they have the newest tablet and a sleek new phone, the audience can assume the character is someone stylish, relevant, and well-to-do.

The type of beverages ordered on-screen work in the same way. If a character orders a vodka martini, the goal is that the audience will take them more seriously and regard the character as upscale. After all, no one thinks of martinis without thinking of James Bond, and no one thinks of Mr. Bond without regarding him as a man of deep sophistication.

Let's take a look at some famous celebrities, movies, and the drinks that were inspired by them.

Drinks & Icons

BOND. JAMES BOND.

What is it about James Bond that makes him such an icon? Many films feature men having high-speed, cliff-hanger adventures in nice suits with fancy cars, but only Bond exudes his uniquely dashing and debonair air when he orders a Vesper

Martini, shaken, not stirred. A sophisticated drink for a sophisticated man. Bond is classic elegance in one handsome package. Iconic. Renowned. Legendary. And the audience holds Mr. Bond in the highest regard.

As vodka snobs, this is our goal: to become iconic in the same way James Bond is iconic. To hold ourselves to a higher standard. To know what we want and to demand it—politely, of course, and with self-assurance and sophistication. And to elevate the way others see us—and the way we feel about ourselves—simply by the way we order our drinks from the bar.

James Bond's Vesper Martini

Instead of ordering a drink from the menu, try this Hollywood twist on a classic martini.

Ingredients
2 ounces gin
1 ounce vodka
½ ounce Kina Lillet

Instructions
1. Combine all ingredients in an ice filled glass.
2. Shake—don't stir!—for a genuine Bond martini, then strain into a chilled glass.
3. Garnish with slice of lemon peel.

CASABLANCA

Is there any movie more classic and wonderful than *Casablanca*? With Humphrey Bogart's famous (and ad-libbed) one-liner "Here's looking at you, kid," *Casablanca* embodies elegance, not only through the grace of Ingrid Bergman but with a cocktail that is high society itself.

When Rick's ex Yvonne brings in a Nazi date who orders a French 75 it's a political affront, but there are few cocktails more elegant than this beautiful friendship of vodka and champagne, called the *Soixante-Quinze* en français. As with many drinks, the origin of the French 75 has a bit of folklore surrounding it.

According to the *Gin Foundry*, the cocktail was named by Scottish-born Harry MacElhone at Harry's American Bar in Paris in 1926, but MacElhone credited Malachy "Pat" McGarry of Buck's Club in London for its creation. MacElhone named this World War I drink after the famous French 75mm Howitzer field gun due to its kick. But if we dig deeper into the origins of the cocktail, we find that our beloved Charles Dickens and other nineteenth century hosts frequently served gin and champagne cups with a similar recipe to their guests.

Another tale is that soldiers created the drink when they ran out of club soda (which would have made the drink a Tom Collins) and substituted champagne. While it is unlikely that the soldiers had champagne but not club soda, it's my favorite French 75 origin story. No matter how the French 75 came to be, *Difford's Guide* states that one commonality among every version all the French 75 origin recipes is that they contained gin.

While a French 75 can be made with gin or cognac, we prefer the vodka variety, as does model Kate Moss. According to Samantha Leal for *Marie Claire*, Moss likes to order them at the Hemingway Bar at the Ritz in Paris, a place I'd very much like to visit, where they call a vodka French 75 a French 76.

No matter how you take your French 75 (or French 76), remember that, like Bogart told Bergman in *Casablanca*, "We'll always have Paris."

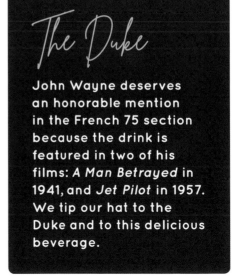

The Duke

John Wayne deserves an honorable mention in the French 75 section because the drink is featured in two of his films: *A Man Betrayed* in 1941, and *Jet Pilot* in 1957. We tip our hat to the Duke and to this delicious beverage.

French 75 (*Soixante-Quinze*)

Ingredients

2 ounces vodka

1 teaspoon superfine sugar

½ ounce lemon juice

Ice

5 ounces chilled champagne

Lemon twist for garnish

Instructions

1. Combine the vodka, sugar, lemon juice, and ice (not the champagne!) in a cocktail shaker.
2. Shake well, ensuring the sugar is dissolved.
3. Strain into a champagne flute.
4. Gently top with the champagne and garnish with a slice of lemon peel. Enjoy!

THE OFFICE

Taking an ungainly leap from a classic of 1942 cinema to a hilarious modern day mockumentary about office workers, we look at vodka beverages in *The Office* with a hat tip to Josh Rosenberg at *Floor 8*'s "Five *The Office* Inspired Cocktails for Your Next Work Party." Whether it's Meredith Palmer getting smashed at the Christmas party and setting her hair on fire or Angela Martin smuggling liquor in a Styrofoam soda cup, fans of the hit show *The Office* will never have to wait long for an alcoholic joke or reference.

In the "Moroccan Christmas" episode (S5, E11), Michael Scott, everyone's favorite boss, believes he creates what many consider to be a vodka staple: the Orange Vod-juice-ka, also known as a Screwdriver. Scott also invents the One of Everything, which includes equal parts scotch, absinthe, rum, gin, vermouth, triple sec, and—of course—two packs of Splenda, his favorite sweetener. We do *not* recommend this drink. It sounds like a death trap.

Not to be outdone, in season six, assistant-to-the-regional-manager Dwight Schrute creates his own beet vodka (S6, E15), which a colleague describes as "farm-boy swill" and which sounds a little terrible. But Dwight may have been onto something. Craft distillery Art in the Age's award-winning Beet Root Vodka makes a delicious base for what we're calling Beets over Rocks, adapted from the Conductor, a "winter Bloody Mary" developed by Al DePompeis at the Society Café in New York via *Tasting Table*. We like to think Dwight was the inspiration.

Dwight's Beets over Rocks

Ingredients

One shot each (or equal parts):

Art in the Age Beet Root Vodka

Purple carrot juice

Pineapple juice

Lemon juice

Ice

Cucumber slice for garnish

Instructions

1. Combine all ingredients in a shaker.

2. Shake well.

3. Pour into tumbler, garnish with cucumber, and enjoy.

Note If you're unable to purchase Art in the Age's beet vodka near you, *Tasting Table* has a recipe for you to make your own. You might want to wear gloves to avoid red stains on your fingers! Peel and grate a beet into a bowl, then cover it with one cup of vodka. Store the mixture sealed in the refrigerator for two days. Shake it after day one, and strain it well before you drink it. Cheers!

GAME OF THRONES

Since many fans of HBO's *Game of Thrones* (*GoT*) may have drunk themselves into a stupor after the disappointing finale, let's check out a couple of cocktails that have been created in the show's honor.

An elevated and gingered up version of the vodka cranberry in honor of *GoT* was submitted to Emma Cooke's BuzzFeed article "Seventeen Cocktails Every *Game of Thrones* Lover Must Try." The strawberry-garnished Ygritte includes 1½ ounces vodka and adds in a tablespoon each of lemon juice and cranberry juice with a splash of ginger ale. The also-delicious-looking Needle, from the same article, submitted by aheapingspoonful.com, consists of two parts vodka to one part ginger beer with freshly squeezed lime juice.

SPOTLIGHT: ICELANDIC MOUNTAIN VODKA

Actor Hafbor Julius Bjornsson (Ser Gregor "The Mountain" Clegane) launched his own vodka in 2016 called Icelandic Mountain Vodka. Distilled seven times and made with pure Icelandic water, this strong spirit comes in with 40 percent alcohol. Check out their website icelandicmountainvodka.is for recipes, including the Bloody Mountain, with their recipe for a rich, thick tomato juice strong enough to stand up in any flavor battle.

SEX AND THE CITY

The first sighting of a Cosmopolitan on the HBO hit *Sex and the City* is in "The Awful Truth" (S2, E2). Carrie Bradshaw (Sarah Jessica Parker) is downing double vodkas on the rocks while a Cosmopolitan, refined and elegant, sits untouched near Samantha (Kim Catrall). The Cosmopolitan was the perfect drink for the show, bringing in sophistication and a beautiful pink color. I think we can all agree the best Cosmo line is when Carrie places an order in a drive-through: "I'd like a cheeseburger, large fries, and a Cosmopolitan."

That sounds amazing, actually.

My favorite Cosmo recipe comes from the Noble Pig, who dubs her version the "World's Best Cosmopolitan." She's a girl after my own heart, with her dedication to top-shelf vodkas for better tasting drinks. The Noble Pig recipe calls for a high-quality citron vodka, and I recommend Florida Cane's Key West Lemon and Lime Vodka. I love it sooooo much!

The World's Best Cosmopolitan

Adapted from the Noble Pig

Ingredients
2½ ounces citron vodka
1 ounce Cointreau
1 ounce cranberry juice
½ ounce lime juice, freshly squeezed
Ice, crushed
Orange peel for garnish

Instructions
1. Combine vodka, Cointreau, cranberry juice, and freshly squeezed lime juice in a cocktail shaker.
2. Shake well.
3. Strain over a fine mesh into a cocktail glass filled with crushed ice. Garnish, sip, enjoy!

How to Be a Vodka Snob

HOW TO GET AWAY WITH MURDER

Fans of the show *How to Get Away with Murder* know that Annalise Keating's favorite drink is vodka, but what even ardent fans might not know is that her vodka of choice *does not exist*! Kelly Schremph followed up on this mystery for *Bustle* and reveals that Kashchey Vodka is named for *Kashchey the Deathless* (also translated as *Kashchey the Immortal*), a Russian opera about an evil wizard who preys on young women, gains immortality, and then is killed in an ironic twist. Does this play's plot somehow foreshadow what will happen to Annalise? You'll have to binge-watch to find out.

How to Get Away with Nothing Vodka Shots

Choose a high-quality vodka when taking shots. One of my faves is ZYR.

Ingredients
Vodka

Instructions
1. Pour a shot. Enjoy.

SPOTLIGHT: ZYR

A shot of vodka needs to be smooth going down and have a crisp taste. My favorite vodka for shots is ZYR, whose website lists numerous accolades from major reviewers and a perfect 100 rating from Wine Enthusiast Magazine. ZYR boasts a 9 • 5 • 3 proprietary formula (see https://zyrvodka.com/pages/art -of-zyr) that leaves their vodka clean, smooth, and creamy. With nine filtrations, five distillations, and three tastings, ZYR is a clear winner and a vodka you'll love to drink.

ARRESTED DEVELOPMENT

Lucille Bluthe (played by Jessica Walter), the snide and savage matriarch of the Bluthe family, leaves us clutching our bellies in laughter as she says whatever comes to her mind and drowns herself in vodka martinis. As Casey Rackham for *Buzzfeed* reminds us in her roundup of hilarious Lucille Bluth quotes, even for breakfast she asks for vodka rocks, with a piece of toast as an afterthought. One of the best lines from *Arrested Development* comes from her daughter Lindsay Funke (Portia de Rosssi). She's hungover from a night of drinking and her brother Michael (Jason Bateman) questions her.

Transcript: "Exit Strategy" (S3, E12):

Michael *And so you just finished off the bottle?*

Lindsay *Well, I had to. It's vodka. It goes bad once it's opened.*

Michael *I think that's another one of Mom's little fibs.*

Ah, Lucille. Fib, indeed. Vodka doesn't really "go bad," it just gets weaker over time. However, according to DoesItGoBad.com, it is possible for bacteria or yeast to develop if the proof gets low enough (as in, the vodka has been sitting around for so long that most of the alcohol has evaporated). So while the vodka you find in the back of the cupboard is probably fine to drink, if it smells weird or has anything floating in it, toss it without regret.

The Man in Black

Adapted from Distillerista.com

Fans of Johnny Cash, Tommy Lee Jones and Will Smith, or WestWorld will enjoy an elevated spin-off of the classic Screwdriver made black by adding activated charcoal. Our take on the Man in Black also includes chocolate bitters and vodka, although the original recipe uses gin.

Ingredients

1½ ounces vodka

⅛ teaspoon activated charcoal

½ ounce orange cordial

3 dashes chocolate bitters

3 dashes orange bitters

Ice

Instructions

1. Combine all ingredients into a shaker cup.
2. Shake well, then double-strain.
3. Garnish with a slice of orange. Enjoy!

Fun Fact

ACTIVATED CHARCOAL

The ancient Egyptians used activated charcoal as far back as 1500 BC. It is still used by people today for whitening teeth, to remove toxins from the body by drinking it, and in hospital emergency rooms to counteract overdoses. Never consume the toxic charcoal remains from a grill or barbeque. Activated charcoal is created from wood or coconut husks and can be purchased in powder or capsule form.

THE BLUES BROTHERS

If you're a fan of John Candy, you might remember his line in *The Blues Brothers*: "Who wants an Orange Whip? Orange Whip? Orange Whip? Three Orange Whips." The name of this delicious drink reminds me of the refreshing Disney Dole Whips we had when we were kids. To have a grown-up variation on a childhood favorite is, at least in my mind, a great reason to add a drink to the rotation.

Orange Whip

Ingredients

4 ounces orange juice

1 ounce rum

1 ounce vodka

2 ounces cream

Orange slices to garnish, optional

Instructions

1. Blend all ingredients together.
2. Pour into a frosty mug and garnish with orange slices.

HOUSE OF CARDS

If there was ever a show full of intrigue, suspicion, and politics, *House of Cards* is at the top of the list. The show gets an honorable mention here for debuting a $1.3 million bottle of Russo-Baltique vodka that celebrated the one hundredth anniversary of the company. The bottle is made of bulletproof glass and the flask is fashioned of radiator guards from actual Russo-Baltique automobiles.

What makes this vodka even more intriguing? A bottle was stolen and found empty in a construction site in Denmark. The owner reclaimed it and declares it's still worth the $1.3 million price tag.

WAY ... WAY OUT (1966)

A second honorable mention goes to a film from the 1960s called *Way . . . Way Out* starring Jerry Lewis. I have great memories of watching Jerry Lewis films with my dad and sister and laughing so hard I couldn't breathe at some of his antics. In *Way . . . Way Out* there is a clip where Lewis is in outer space with a Russian who teaches him how to make instant vodka with a powder capsule and water.

Lewis ends up chugging the powder (the vodka!), drinking water from a hose, and then shaking himself like you would shake a cocktail. It's too ridiculous for words, but I love that I'm able to honor this memory of childhood comedies with you.

TOURS, TASTINGS, AND TRAVEL

Distillery tours and tastings are not just for a guys' night out or for booze-brand fanboys. Arranging a sampling or scheduling a tour from a local distillery is a great plan for an intoxicating date night, a fun event with friends, or even a memorable girls' night out. Tours and tastings are also perfect opportunities to sample and purchase your next favorite vodka.

Jay's first vodka distillery tour was located just a few miles from our home. He found a Groupon, called a friend, and boom!

In Jay's words:

I didn't know what to expect, but upon entering the showroom, my reservations were calmed. We were in an attractive space surrounded by an amazing display of custom wood furniture. The host showed us to a table with two seats, and as the other guests arrived, made sure that everyone was introduced.

After the initial greetings were over, my first vodka distillery tour and official tasting had begun. Since this was a relatively new brand and the still was small, the tour was led by one of the co-owners and distillers, which gave a personal feel and sense of connection. They were able to describe the struggles they went through early on and how they were able to overcome those obstacles. Along with that sense of community, I learned so much about the distilling process and what made their brand unique.

Perhaps my favorite part, and the most memorable, was that I got to be face-to-face with the passion behind one of my new favorite vodka brands. I absolutely encourage you to take advantage of tastings and tours. If you're on vacation, see if there are any distilleries in the area or if any liquor stores have events that coincide with your visit.

Tastings

Another great way to experience the amazing flavors and flair of various vodkas is through tasting events hosted at your nearby liquor stores and distilleries. These demonstrations provide brands an opportunity to showcase their products and reach a new customer base.

Larger liquor stores and chain stores may offer tastings of several brands at once, while smaller stores may choose to showcase one or two brands. From the vodka appreciator's perspective, tasting events are great ways to gain knowledge of new offerings from brands you may know and an even better way to taste new, up-and-coming brands.

I recommend you absorb the knowledge of the vendors, note their selections, and take the opportunity to ask questions. They are invested in their product and want their vodkas to be well received.

When Jay traveled through Singapore, he attended a tasting event that included a carefully curated international vodka section. Many of the vodkas showcased were brands that we have here in the United States but had never tried. He was able to sample a variety of top-notch vodkas and come home with some great recommendations. His favorite find from the show was Haku vodka, which is now in regular rotation as part of our personal vodka collection.

BENEFITS

Many tasting events are held year-round and on a regular basis, but pay attention to specials, particularly before holidays, local events, or major weekend happenings. The beauty of local tastings is that you get a lot of the knowledge that you would from a distillery tour, but without traveling a long distance. But perhaps the best part of a reseller-hosted tasting event is that the featured distributors will usually provide a substantial discount as an incentive to purchase their brand. Call your local liquor stores to see when their next liquor tasting is being held.

Tastings and tours give you the opportunity to learn about new drinks and to expand your palate beyond your normal drink of choice. You'll also often learn fun and quirky facts and behind-the-scenes news about the distilleries. In fact, I would be willing to bet that even the most vodka-snobby person on your friends list will walk away with some new knowledge or inspiration to make the tour worthwhile.

Of course, the best benefit of attending tastings is being able to spend time with family and friends. Be sure to snap some great Instagram-worthy group photos and make some memories. They last much longer than a bottle of vodka.

COSTS

Distillery tour hosts have a vast knowledge of their brand and often offer a broad range of samples and sips, so tour-goers will likely be charged a few dollars. The majority of tours or tastings that I have attended over the last decade have ranged in price from $10 all the way up to $30. This may seem steep, but consider the knowledge you will gain and also the discounts, samples, and any other premiums offered for the price of admission. Typically, the more expensive events include a bottle or some other souvenir to take home.

PRODUCT KNOWLEDGE

Small distilleries will utilize someone from the production line to lead the tour, but larger brands have specific public relations people in charge of their tours. Tour guides are well-versed in their brand as well as other brands. Since tours are more fun when they are interactive, feel free to mention to the guide your favorite things about their brand or, in a discrete way, features you appreciate in other brands. After all, guides are also salespeople. They should be able to guide you to the product of theirs you will most enjoy and explain where their brand excels.

JAY'S TASTING ADVICE: TRY SOMETHING NEW

I once had the opportunity to tour one of the largest beer makers' factories, and we were given loads of free samples. Since I'm really not a beer fan, I slightly tasted the two beers that intrigued me and then passed the rest to my friends. The tour guide noticed and asked if everything was all right. So, on the spot, I explained that the beer was fine, but I don't really like beer.

There was a chuckle in the room from the other guests, so I explained that I enjoyed the art and science aspect of it all, and thankfully, the tour continued. It was a bit embarrassing, but the people on the tour were also interested in the process, so I enjoyed the rest of the event without feeling awkward.

Aside from some gaining some great alcohol-making knowledge and acquiring some practical drinking tips, I had a great time and it was worth the price of admission. The lesson from all of this: don't be afraid to try something new.

LOCAL DISTILLERIES

An advantage to touring local distilleries is that you may find special brands or flavors that are not available anywhere else. Since vodka is not aged like whiskeys or bourbons, there are several distilleries that have a special line that is produced for onsite purchase only.

Hangar One markets a Distiller's Exclusive line that features seasonally rotated small-batch vodkas only available from their facilities.

Middle West spirits, which produces OYO brand vodka, is one of the brands that offer tours of their working distillery floors. I had the opportunity to taste some of OYO's finely crafted product when I was in the Ohio area a number of years ago for a family gathering. Looking back, I wish I had taken the hour-long tour to learn more about this particular brand.

Fun fact

Hangar One brand is housed inside of an old World War II hangar, which is really cool.

While travelling through Tennessee a few years ago to visit family, we happened to stay at a hotel that was rather close to some distilleries. Even though we weren't able to take an actual tour, I was able to buy a few bottles of liquor from their gift shop that were not available outside of the state. In fact, this has happened on multiple occasions, which makes for a great story when you share that vodka with friends.

The majority of liquor laws are still in place from the Prohibition era and thus constrain the sale of liquor from county to county, as well as from state to state, so keep an eye out for locally crafted vodkas when you travel.

SAMPLES

When touring distilleries, it is common to be given various samples of their craft. Most of these tasting samples will be room temperature. At room temperature, the flavor profiles of the vodka will stand out. When a vodka is chilled to low temperatures, the flavor profile is less noticeable and the texture and mouthfeel become more apparent.

CREATE YOUR OWN TOUR EXPERIENCE

If you are not in a location where you can get a tour of a distillery, then do what we did a few months ago: map out your own vodka-themed bar tour! Jay and I selected a few upscale bars and restaurants in our local area and then set out on our version of a progressive dinner.

Our first stop was a locally owned liquor store known for samples and tasting events. We spent about thirty minutes tasting samples of various vodkas before heading to stop number two—food! We chose a small eatery that had one, and only one, vodka-based drink on the menu: an extremely spicy Bloody Mary. It turned out to be the best Bloody Mary ever. We shared the blazing tomato drink and an appetizer before we departed for our next destination—a chic, high-end restaurant we had wanted to try. Their coffee-vodka dessert drink and classic Moscow Mule were utter perfection. The bar's atmosphere was great, but we had one more stop to go.

Our final destination was an Irish pub just a few blocks from home. That pub had only one vodka-based drink on the menu and it came with a surprising twist: a dirty martini with a potato wedge garnish. We ate dinner, sipped the martini (sans potato wedge) and called it a night. It was truly one of the best date nights ever, and a relatively inexpensive way to spend an evening.

Jay and I loved trying these new drinks and ranking them in order of our favorites. Some drinks we loved, others we did not. This date night was a

great way to experience different local bars and eateries, and it felt great to be supporting local businesses. It was a unique experience that I'm eager to repeat. If you have your own version of this progressive vodka-tasting dinner, I'd love to hear about it!

SPOTLIGHT: FLORIDA CANE VODKA

The brand began in a rebellious, less-than-legal manner in a South Tampa garage using three Miller Lite beer cans and a pressure cooker for a still. After two years of planning and plotting, the company was hatched in February of 2012 in a small industrial storage unit.

Florida Cane Distillery has worked with local officials to help modernize distillation in the state of Florida. Florida Cane vodka is all distilled from South Florida sugar cane. They don't claim their success rests on their mash mixture or the quality of their yeast strain but rather on their filtration system. After extensive searching, they landed on coconut husks.

Each batch of Florida Cane's vodka is filtered over the course of two weeks through 90 feet of activated carbon from coconut husks. Their dedication to perfection pays off with an award winning, crisp-and-clean vodka that regularly finds its way into my home bar. Florida Cane also features another favorite spirit of mine—moonshine. Their moonshine is the highest proof in the state of Florida at 109. In 2016, the brand relocated their distillery into a historic building in Ybor city.

We applaud the team over at Florida Cane Distillery for their commitment to excellence, their legislative work, and their amazing customer service. Be sure to check them out in person or online at www.floridacane.com

HOSTESSING AND HOLIDAYS

What's a party without a special drink menu? To be the host or hostess with the mostest, you'll find cocktails (and their alcohol-less virgin counterparts, the mocktails) to be a great addition to any get-together.

Not only does having a signature drink add a sense of specialness to the event, but gatherings can be awkward, especially for the introverted among us, and having an elegant drink to hold and sip gives guests something to do with their hands.

A fun idea is to create a special drink for your event, which can be named after the guest of honor. For example, in the hit TV series *Gilmore Girls*, the Rory Cocktail was created to celebrate Rory Gilmore's twenty-first birthday. The girly Rory Cocktail is supposed to be extra pink and overly sweet, so our version is lightened up a bit, but the concept of a special drink remains a great one.

I might not be the hostess that Rory's grandmother Emily Gilmore is, but let's explore some fun and festive holiday recipes with a few hostessing tips thrown in for fun!

You can find some great ideas and tips on how to make your own pineapple vodka and pink sugar for the rim of a Rory Cocktail over at ATipsyGiraffe.com. We've included a link to her recipe for this beautiful cocktail in the Further Reading section, but we hope you'll enjoy our own adaption as well.

Add to your calendar: National Vodka Day is October 4.

The Rory Cocktail

Ingredients

2 ounces pineapple vodka

4½ ounces champagne or prosecco

¼ teaspoon grenadine

Instructions

1. Combine the vodka and grenadine in a shaker and shake well.

2. Pour over ice into a chilled martini glass.

3. Add the champagne and serve!

To Punch or Not to Punch

While we're on the topic of drinks and television, on the hit TV sitcom *Frasier*, a show about elitist psychologist and Seattle radio host Frasier Crane, Frasier and his brother Niles most often drink wine or a glass of sherry. We see vodka mentioned in the episode "The Fight Before Christmas 2" (S7, E11), however, when Frasier's producer Roz returns his extravagant silver punch bowl which she borrowed to make her holiday beverage.

Frasier *"What kind of punch did you serve?"*

Roz *"Well, first I filled it with ice. Then I just poured orange juice and vodka over it."*

Frasier *"Well, Roz, that's just a giant screwdriver!"*

Roz *"Yeah, so? What am I, Martha Stewart?"*

As a nod to Frasier and Niles, here's a swankier vodka and sherry punch recipe from Barbara Mealey's *Potent Punches*. It's sure to please the taste buds of the upper classes at any holiday gathering.

Magnificent Punch

Ingredients

1 quart vodka

1 quart light sherry (not too dry)

½ cup maraschino juice

1 cup curaçao

4 quarts or 5 fifths
champagne, chilled

2 quarts club soda, chilled
(2 28-ounce bottles plus 1 cup)

Instructions

1. Combine first four ingredients
   and pour into punch bowl. At
   serving time, carefully pour
   in champagne and soda.

Yield 44 6-ounce servings.

Note Punch is extremely
smooth but very potent.

Spring and Summer Parties

Whether you're hosting a neighborhood barbecue or back-to-school bash, the spring and summer seasons are great times to revel in new beginnings, cool off with refreshing cocktails, and get in touch with your inner child.

When we decided to plan a party during the hot, sweaty month of July, we wanted to stay away from drinks that seemed heavy and instead focus on drinks that make it into the summer-and-fun category with their fruity flavors.

Lite beers work fairly well for most fun-in-the-sun gatherings, but since I'm just a bit of an elitist (and since I was in the middle of finishing this book) I decided to stick with vodka-themed drinks. Our guests were also bringing drinks to the party, so this kept cost down and made a fun drink station to work from.

A few simple ingredients afforded us loads of drink-mixing enjoyment, kept people from intoxication, and allowed all the guests who didn't know each other to mingle harmoniously. As hosts, we had a DIY mojito and Moscow Mule station, which was an unintended conversation starter that helped people mingle. It definitely "broke the ice" (#badpun).

As part of our lifestyle-diet, my husband and I try to stay as low-carb as possible, so we chose diet versions of the ginger beer and had diet sodas on hand. We also elected not to use Rose's lime juice, which is often called for in cocktails. We substituted erythritol, which we had on hand (we like Swerve), and lime juice.

OUR SHOPPING LIST

- Diet ginger beer
- Quality vodkas (we picked up a lime version as well as "plain")
- Fresh mint leaves
- Limes
- Lemon juice (plastic container from the produce aisle)
- Diet tonic water
- Club soda

We mixed up some Moscow Mules as well as some fresh mint Mojitos. Having never played bartenders to a crowd before, we chose these drinks because they are easy to make and always well received. Since vodka is a neutral spirit, it mixed seamlessly with flavored waters, refreshing juices, and a variety of other ingredients. And because we purchased local vodkas, we were able to discuss what we liked about the distillery and some fun facts we learned during our private tour earlier in the summer.

The first drink that we peddled out to the masses at our poolside barbeque was the Vodka Mojito—a classy and refreshing cocktail that is perfect for a sunny summer afternoon. We offered this beverage in classic and sugar-free versions.

HOSTING TIP:
AN OUNCE OF PREVENTION

When hosting a party for both kids and adults, buy cups in two sizes and colors. We broke our "no Solo® cup" rule for our summer holiday bash and chose smaller blue cups for the kiddos and larger red ones for the adults. Even though we had markers out to label people's names, it was a safer way to ensure that young mouths didn't accidentally sip from an alcoholic cup.

To create the Vodka Mojitos, my hubs mushed (muddled) about four mint leaves and about two grams of stevia in the bottom of a red plastic party cup. He filled the cup with ice cubes, then added about one cup of cold club soda over the mint, ice, and stevia. Rounding out the drink, he added a shot of Florida Cane Key Lime vodka and about two tablespoons of lime juice and then stirred briefly with a straw. Finally, he split a lime slice on the side as a garnish.

It may sound complicated, but the drink took less than a minute to make, and it was delish. The trick was fresh mint and quality vodka. Simple, classic drinks can set the tone for an upscale pool party.

Sugar-Free Mojito

Ingredients

4 fresh mint leaves

2 tablespoons lime juice

2 grams stevia or erythritol (we used packets of Swerve)

1 ounce premium vodka

1 cup of club soda

1 fresh lime

crushed ice

Instructions

1. Muddle the mint leaves in the bottom of a glass with the lime juice and Stevia (or erythritol).

2. Add ice and club soda.

3. Add vodka and stir.

4. Garnish with lime slice and serve.

Note You can make this as a regular vodka mojito by replacing the 2 grams of stevia with about 1 tablespoon simple syrup (again, adjust to personal preference).

SPOTLIGHT:
RUSSIAN STANDARD VODKA

LABELS INCLUDE RUSSIAN STANDARD ORIGINAL, RUSSIAN STANDARD GOLD, RUSSIAN STANDARD PLATINUM, AND IMPERIA.

The elite of Russian Standard's labels, Imperia Vodka, is said to follow a recipe created for Tsar Alexander III in 1894. Imperia Vodka is made with winter wheat and soft, high-quality water from Russia's Lake Ladoga, which is the largest lake in Europe.

Inspired by Dmitri Mendeleev, the inventor of the periodic table, Russian Standard vodka is a balanced spirit with the perfect water to alcohol ratio. The vodka is filtered through charcoal and beautiful white quartz crystal, and the facility boasts large stainless-steel columns that trap impurities.

Russian Standard Vodka intrigues us because of their mission, stated prominently on their website, to bring affordable luxury to everyone. With four labels under their brand, you can find a 750 ml bottle of Russian Standard Original for less than $19 at most wine and liquor stores. On the other end of the scale, bottles of Imperia will cost you $30 or more.

Strawberry Moscow Mule

Fresh strawberries are one of God's greatest gifts. Our family loves to visit the Plant City Strawberry Festival, where the strawberries are ripe, juicy, and absolutely scrumptious. In the south, strawberries are often harvested in April, making them the perfect fruit for a blissful springtime . . . and cocktail recipes.

Ingredients

1½ ounces premium vodka

3 strawberries

½ ounce of lime juice

½ cup of regular or diet ginger beer

Fresh lime, sliced

Instructions

1. Muddle 2 strawberries in the bottle of a glass or copper mug.
2. Add the vodka and ginger beer.
3. Squeeze lime juice over the top.
4. Stir briefly, and then garnish with lime wedge and strawberry.

Fun Fact

Ginger beer, as opposed to ginger ale, is used in our Moscow Mule recipes. According to the *Huffington Post*'s Kitchen Daily, there is a huge difference between ginger beers and ginger ales. A ginger ale is simply ginger-flavored carbonated water, which has a light, more mellow taste, while ginger beer is brewed and fermented, giving it a stronger, spicier finish. Despite the fermentation, there is less than .05 percent alcohol content in a ginger beer, which does not exceed the FDA requirements for non-alcoholic beverages.

And for our guests who love coffee but hate to drink it when it's smoldering hot outside, here's a quick java punch from Barbara Mealey's *Potent Punches*. Served over ice it will keep your guests cool . . . and caffeinated.

Troika Special

Ingredients

1 ounce lemon juice

1 ounce vodka

1 small jigger of Tia Maria or other coffee liqueur

1 small jigger Cointreau or other orange liqueur

Instructions

1. Combine all ingredients and serve over ice. For more servings increase all ingredients equally.

Yield 1 serving.

St. Patrick's Day

I'd be doing a great disservice to my Irish roots if I dove right into summer punches and didn't mention one of the biggest drinking days of the year. This minty concoction from Barbara Mealey's *Potent Punches* will leave you with the luck o' the Irish. Be sure to wear something green, so you don't get pinched!

Crème de Menthe

Ingredients

1 cup sugar

1 cup water

2 cups vodka

¼ cup white corn syrup

6 drops oil of mint, not essence (sold in drugstores)

Instructions

1. Boil sugar and water until sugar is dissolved. Add rest of ingredients and bottle. Ready to drink in approximately one week.

Note May add green food coloring if desired.

Yield 1 quart.

WHAT DO ABV AND PROOF MEAN?

When hosting a party, it's a good idea to know the alcohol content in the beverages you are serving and drinking. As food writer Amy Reiter explains in her article "Why Alcohol Content Is Measured in 'Proof'" for the Food Network, throughout history there have been several ways to measure (and tax) alcohol content. Currently the most common in the United States is based on proof. The term *proof* originally came from sixteenth-century England and the gunpowder test, where an official would soak gunpowder with the alcohol in question and try to ignite it. If the gunpowder lit, then the liquor had enough alcohol to burn, and it was taxed as a "proof spirit." This quick-and-dirty proof test was abandoned in the early 1800s for a more scientific method that measured alcohol by volume (abv), which is now the international standard. Proof is still used as a measure in the United States, however, where it now means double the alcohol by volume number. The ethanol in liquor is less dense than water, but it is "suspended" in water. Hence the alcohol by volume (abv) being half of its proof. Combining the alcohol and water in your liquor first makes it easier to add to and mix with water-based mixers.

The other drink that we featured at our summer soiree was the Sugar-Free Moscow Mule. This drink maintained the lightness of our beverages for the day but provided a slightly more robust drink as we edged nearer to fireworks time. This drink also catered to our guests who normally drink sodas without requiring us to purchase additional ingredients. The only other thing we needed to purchase was diet ginger beer (or regular, if so inclined). The same rules applied for this drink as for all of our other drinks: Jay and I made one or two of them for our guests, and then we left the ingredients and a recipe card for them to make their own according to their taste and refill requirements.

If you're having a party in summer, during the height of fresh-fruit season, adding a fruit-based cocktail or punch to your party offerings is always a hit. What could be more cooling than frozen watermelon and cucumber?

SUMMER WATERSLIDE SLUSH

Recipe adapted from Thug Kitchen's Watermelon Cucumber Slushie

Ingredients

3 pounds of seedless watermelon, diced and frozen

½ cup skinned, chopped cucumber

Juice from 1 lime (about 2 tablespoons)

8–10 fresh mint leaves or a couple of drops of mint extract

¼ cup coconut water

½ cup vodka of your choice

1 teaspoon agave, maple syrup, or honey (optional)

Instructions

1. Remove the rind and dice the watermelon into chunks, removing any seeds. Freeze for a minimum of four hours.

2. Add frozen watermelon chunks to the rest of the ingredients in a blender.

3. Blend until smooth. Add sweetener to taste.

4. Pour your slush into a fancy-ass glass, or grab a tumbler and enjoy. Raised pinky optional.

SPOTLIGHT: VAN GOGH VODKA

Vincent Van Gogh said, "I often think that the night is more alive and more richly colored than the day." And when the night is paired with great-tasting spirits, who can help but have their own spirits lifted?

Van Gogh brand flavored vodkas are rich and vibrant, just like their namesake's paintings. Hand-crafted in Holland, Van Gogh vodka is a multi-distilled grain alcohol that goes through what they call an "all-natural double infusion flavoring process." With over twenty flavors, multiple awards, and several OU kosher certified flavors, Van Gogh vodka earned a feature in *KosherEye* and is a great addition to the cocktail mixes you crave.

When I was in college, I got to try my first fresh-from-the-farm Georgia peach. My friends and I went to a roadside stand and purchased a bag. They smelled incredible, and the first juicy bite into the soft, tender flesh was everything I'd hoped it would be. Canned peaches can work in a pinch in a lot of recipes, but I'll be honest: fresh peaches are worth waiting for.

PEACH FLUFF

This frosty, tangy cocktail from Barbara Mealey's *Potent Punches* is perfect for a small mid-summer get-together, when days are hot and peaches are fresh and sweet.

Ingredients

1 6-ounce can frozen lemonade

6 ounces vodka

2 whole peaches, fresh and unpeeled, but pitted

5 ice cubes (approximately)

Instructions

1. Place all ingredients into a blender and mix well. Serve in frosted Old Fashioned glasses.

Yield 5 4-ounce servings.

Hello, Summer! PB&J Cocktail

Recipe adapted from Jonathan Pogash's "Nuts & Berries" cocktail in Alicia French's SheKnows "Peanut Butter and Jelly Cocktail Recipes"

Peanut butter and jelly are not just for kids anymore. Grab a frosty mug and enjoy a grown-up twist on a childhood favorite treat. Just a head's up: PB&J vodka tastes much better mixed than as an individual shot.

Ingredients

½ ounce Van Gogh PB&J Vodka

¾ ounce berry liquor

¾ ounce cream

Ice

Instructions

1. Add ingredients to cocktail shaker.
2. Shake well.
3. Strain.
4. Garnish with berries and sip away!

Notes This delicious treat can be transformed into a milkshake as well, also available in Alicia French's PB&J recipes for SheKnows. Nadia G, star of the Cooking Channel's "Nadia G's Bitchin' Kitchen" substitutes one tablespoon of raspberries for the berry liquor, one cup of milk for the cream, and adds one half a banana, one overflowing tablespoon of peanut butter, and one half-cup of vanilla ice cream. Blend and serve with remaining fruit for a delicious treat.

And if you're feeling generous, leave out the vodka and whip up a batch for the littles in your life. Enjoy!

Fun Fact

April 2 is National Peanut Butter and Jelly Day.

Fall and Winter Parties

Fall brings crisp autumn air, football, and changing leaves, and the winter months are full of snow angels, ciders, carols, and gifts. At the heart of it all, however, the fall and winter months are all about family. However you're entertaining this year, enjoy these recipes with those you love most.

WASSAIL

Wassail was introduced to me by the sitcom *Frasier* as an alternative to Roz's previously mentioned giant holiday Screwdriver. In "We Two Kings" (S10, E10), it is Niles and Daphne's turn to ask to borrow Frasier's wassail bowl, only to find out Frasier has already loaned it out to a mandrel-caroling group.

What is a mandrel-caroling group? And why did they need a wassail bowl? And what is wassail, anyway? A mandrel is a tool used in lathe-work or forging, so how it could be connected to caroling, I'm not sure. But the definition of wassail sparked an interesting debate in the Crane household.

Niles asks for the wassail bowl. Frasier says he's loaned it. And then Martin, Frasier and Niles' father (and also my favorite character next to Niles), chimes in.

Martin *"Why not just borrow the punch bowl?"*

Frasier *"Because then it wouldn't be wassail, it would be punch."*

Martin *"What's the difference?*

Daphne *"Me dad used to say that punch would make you want to kiss the donkey in the manger scene and wassail makes you want to check into the inn."*

Without a doubt, the best line of the episode is delivered by Martin just a few minutes later. The wassail debate has ended, so we think. While Daphne, Niles, and Frasier debate about who is going to host the festivities that year, Martin stands at the desk, glasses on, and loudly reads, "Wassail . . . a Christmas punch," then shuts the dictionary, smug as you please.

Makes me laugh. Every. Single. Time.

To me, it had always seemed that wassail must have a strong alcoholic content, so I investigated and found out that wassail is a cider-based beverage that originally contained, of all things, curdled cream. A typical wassail bowl can hold a *lot* of liquid—up to ten gallons—and is usually made of pewter or silver.

You may recall a traditional Christmas carol that includes lines about people going a-wassailing among the leaves so green. During a party, the wassail bowl would be brought in with grand ceremony, a carol would be sung, and then the delicious beverage would be served to guests. Many times this ritual was on New Year's Eve, but the wealthy could afford to drink wassail for all twelve days of Christmas. Recipes for wassail can be a little intense, but here's a simpler recipe for wassail that can be enjoyed this holiday season.

Wassail

Adapted from FarmFlavor.com's Traditional Wassail recipe

Ingredients

½ cup vodka

1 gallon apple cider

2 cups orange juice

1 cup lemon juice

½ cup sugar

2 teaspoons cinnamon

1 teaspoon cloves

1 teaspoon nutmeg

1 orange, sliced

Instructions

1. Combine all ingredients (except orange slices) in a large pot.

2. Slowly bring mixture to a boil, then boil for 1 minute.

3. Reduce heat and simmer for 30 minutes.

4. Garnish with orange slices. Serve immediately.

Note Some wassail recipes call for brandy or add cranberry juice or pineapple juice.

Appetizers

With all of those delicious drink recipes, we need complementary snacks to munch on! Appetizers are crucial to any gathering. Some go-to dish ideas include:

- **Charcuterie** Meat and cheese boards are simple to assemble. Choose a selection of deli meats to roll up and display along with cheese squares or cubes. Add olives, grapes, crackers, and your favorite dip or hummus for a wide variety of flavors.

- **Finger sandwiches** I have always loved the triangle-shaped party sandwiches full of egg salad, tuna, ham salad, and—my ultimate favorite!—pimento cheese. You can also slice sub sandwiches into small portions

- **Warm dips** Cream cheese makes an excellent base for many warm dips. Crack Dip is such a hit in our house that I have to make double batches for holidays and parties. Serve with tortilla chips and indulge! Find my recipe below!

- **Wings** Wings are always a hit at parties. You can sub (or complement) the wings with other styles of chicken. Nuggets or popcorn chicken are great options for the younger crowd. Serve your chicken with a few different types of sauces to please every palette, and you've got yourself a winner!

In addition to all these great basics, we like to whip up jalapeño poppers for our guests to snack on, and they're always gone in no time. Poppers are so quick and easy to make from scratch. Enjoy!

Bacon Jalapeño Poppers

Ingredients

Fresh jalapeños (I use about fourteen small ones)

1 8-ounce package cream cheese, softened

1 package real chopped bacon (although fresh crumbled bacon is better!)

Instructions

1. Preheat the oven to 350 degrees.

2. Leaving stems attached, slice jalapeños in half lengthwise, then use a spoon to remove seeds and all inner membranes. The more seeds and membranes you remove, the less heat they will have. Reserve halved jalapeños on a plate or dish.

3. Wash all pepper juices and pieces off your hands.

4. Diligently and thoroughly mix the bacon pieces with a block of softened cream cheese.

5. Spoon the cream cheese and bacon filling into the jalapeño halves. Fill the peppers to slightly over the top and place on cookie sheet or baking dish. The oven will melt down the cream cheese and drop the level a little bit, and heating will also provide a more balanced flavor.

6. Pop the peppers into a preheated oven for about 30 minutes (sometimes a bit longer depending on the number of peppers). You want the tops to be slightly browned.

7. Remove from oven and let cool slightly before transferring to serving dish. Enjoy!

Brittany and Jay's Favorite Crack Dip

There are endless versions of Crack Dip, but after several test runs this is the version we love the best. For 2–4 people (including leftovers), I would halve the recipe. Calories not calculated!

Ingredients

2 blocks cream cheese, softened

2 10-ounce cans Ro*Tel chili and tomatoes, your choice of flavor

2 packets of ranch dressing seasoning

1 10-ounce bag frozen corn, thawed

2 4-ounce cans diced green chilis

1 bag (2 cups) shredded cheddar or Colby Jack cheese (can use more if desired)

¼ pound bacon, fried and drained, or 1 4.3-ounce package of chopped bacon. Use as much or as little as you want!

Optional garnish toppings
diced jalapeños, crumbled bacon, shredded cheese

Instructions for Oven Preparation

1. Pre-heat the oven to 350°.

2. In a large mixing bowl, combine all the ingredients and mix well. If possible, use a mixer or hand mixer to ensure the Ranch seasoning packet is well incorporated.

3. Spoon mixture into a 9×13–inch pan.

4. Bake at 350° for 30–40 minutes, checking often after the 30-minute mark. The top should be slightly brown and bubbly.

5. Serve with tortilla chips or veggie sticks.

Notes For a prettier top, reserve some of the shredded cheese to sprinkle on top before baking. You can also add diced jalapeños or chopped bacon to the top for garnish.

Instructions for Crockpot or Slow Cooker Preparation

1. In a crockpot or slow cooker, combine all the ingredients.

2. Set timer for three hours. Please note: depending on your slow cooker, times can vary.

3. Stir frequently to incorporate all ingredients until smooth.

4. Garnish with diced jalapeños or chopped bacon. Serve with tortilla chips or veggie sticks.

SPECIAL OCCASIONS CALL FOR CAVIAR

The first time I ever tasted caviar I was at a Red Cross Ball at the famous Breakers Hotel in Palm Beach. The ticket prices were way out of my budget, but I was a happy plus-one with my date. I dressed as fancily as I could, and when I walked into the ballroom it was brimming with freshly cut red roses spilling out of urns and vases everywhere. Gorgeous!

Part of the appetizer course contained caviar. This variety was dark, with teeny-tiny eggs served on crostini slices. Bravely, my date and I spooned a little portion onto the bread slices. Together we raised our caviar crostini and took a bite. I closed my eyes to really savor the flavor. Salty. I placed the half-bitten hors d'oeuvre on my plate, swallowed, and took a sip of lemon water.

I can't say that caviar was my favorite appetizer, but I would hope that my palette has matured over the last decade. While caviar may not be on every US menu for Christmas, according to *Gala in the Kitchen*'s blogpost "How to Serve and Garnish Caviar Russian Style," when it comes to holidays in Russia, caviar and vodka are normal fare. The trick is having a healthy amount of butter, which some swear lessens the effects of the vodka as the oils line the stomach and slow down the absorption of the alcohol. I don't recommend overdrinking, so in no way am I condoning eating a slab of butter simply to be able to drink more. Still, butter, particularly some creamy Irish Kerrygold, might be tasty with caviar. So for that buttery flavor alone, spread it thick!

Caviar Appetizer

Ingredients

Caviar (I'd spring for the best brand I could afford!)

Butter

Bread of choice
crostini, baguette, sliced bread

Instructions

1. Grab some bread.
2. Spread on the butter.
3. Spoon some caviar on top. Enjoy!

Desserts

What's a party without something sweet? Try this elegant tiramisu that will sure to be a delight for any event.

Galina's Vodka Tiramisu

Adapted from CookingWithVodka.blogs.com

Ingredients

8 eggs, with yolks and whites separated

⅓ cup sugar

I pound mascarpone

1 cup heavy cream

2 cups espresso, cooled

1 cup vodka

1 cup espresso vodka or Kahlua

30 ladyfingers

2 ounces bittersweet chocolate, grated

¼ cup cocoa powder

Note You'll need multiple bowls!

Instructions

1. Separate the egg yolks and egg whites.

2. Blend the sugar into the egg yolks.

3. Slowly add the mascarpone to the egg yolk mixture.

4. Mix until smooth. Set aside.

5. In a separate bowl, beat the whipping cream until stiff peaks form. Set aside.

6. In yet another bowl, beat the egg whites until stiff peaks form.

7. Gently fold the whipped cream and beaten egg whites into the egg mixture.

8. Combine the cooled espresso, the unflavored vodka, and espresso vodka (or Kahlua) in a large mixing bowl.

9. Spread about ⅓ of the egg / whipped cream mixture along the bottom of a 4–6 quart glass baking dish.

10. Individually soak each ladyfinger in the vodka mixture and gently place in baking dish over layer of egg / whipped cream mixture.

11. Lay the soaked ladyfingers side by side to cover the bottom of the dish.

12. Top with grated chocolate.

13. Place another ⅓ of egg / whipped cream mixture on top of soaked ladyfingers and repeat step 10.

14. Top with remaining grated chocolate followed by remaining egg/whipped cream and dust with cocoa powder.

15. Chill in refrigerator for 2 hours or until set.

Note Serve on dessert plates or in martini glasses for a festive twist.

For individual servings As an alternative to the method above, you can layer the ladyfingers with the egg/whipped cream mixture and grated chocolate in individual serving dishes and chill.

Ladyfinger tip The only tricky part of this recipe is when soaking the ladyfingers in the vodka mixture. Support the ladyfinger fully with your fingers so that it absorbs as much liquid as possible but does not disintegrate before you can lay in in the baking dish. Enjoy!

Fun Fact

Ladyfingers are light, crispy, and sweet cookies or cakes roughly shaped like a large finger. In the UK they may be called trifle sponges or boudoir biscuits.

VODKA AND ANIMALS

Drunken Dancing Bears

Vodka has some history with the four-footed, beloved-yet-ferocious animals we love to cuddle and snuggle with as kiddos, but it's not always a happy history. In news almost too crazy to be true, about eighty bears were kept intoxicated for many years for public amusement in Ukraine. According to May Wilkerson for TheFix.com, Ukraine's Environmental Minister Mykola Zlochevsky spoke out against tolerating animal torture in restaurants where drunken guests make bears drink vodka for laughs.

It's hard to believe in a time when we've worked to be environmentally conscious as a society that something like pouring moonshine down the throats of helpless animals has been allowed. It seems that when Kiev hosted the 2012 EuroSoccer tournament, all eyes were on Ukraine and the backlash from tourists witnessing this monstrosity was enough to raise awareness and put a stop to it. In a 2012 *Deadspin* article, Sean Newell reported that these "vodka bears" were set to be released from their bear rehab into a neighboring forest. In 2017, Iain Burns reported for the *Daily Mail* that the last Ukrainian dancing bear was rescued and taken to live in a bear sanctuary. Godspeed, bears. May you live as God intended.

Ukraine, however, is not the first country to get their bears drunk. Bulgaria, Serbia, Turkey, and Romania have also retired alcoholic teddies. Sadly, dancing bears can trace their roots all the way to back to when they were required for imperial processions, and they were not limited to Eastern Europe. And, sadly, some bear "entertainment" were even worse. According to master's student Pelin Tünaydin, "Another form of exhibiting bears in England was bear baiting, namely the practice of chaining a bear to a pole and siccing a pack of aggressive dogs on it to watch them fight each other to death. This may in fact have been a more fashionable pastime."

The only drunken dancing bears I want to see are the fruit-flavored gummy variety. Whip up a batch of these delightful treats and awaken the kid inside of you.

Drunken Gummy Bears

Adapted from MixThatDrink.com

Ingredients
Vodka
Gummy bears (or gummy worms)

Instructions
1. While soaking the gummies in vodka and leaving them refrigerated for days is common practice, the great people at MixThatDrink.com share a much faster method. Leaving the gummies in a bowl on the counter (as opposed to refrigerated) means a much shorter soak time. Their advice is to use an inexpensive vodka versus a premium brand to save on costs; the taste won't come through strongly enough to make a difference.

2. And while you can, of course, use whatever vodka you choose, their vodka recommendations for gummy bears that don't get mushy are Svedka and Smirnoff. My advice: make sure to buy a brand where you'll enjoy drinking the leftovers!

WHERE'S THE BEAR?

In an effort to bring attention to the plight of polar bear extinction, Polar Ice Vodka has released a limited-edition bottle with their iconic polar bear missing from the label. According to their website, 60 percent of the estimated 26,000 polar bears live in Canada. These bears rely on the ice for food and shelter, but climate change is reducing their habitat.

To raise awareness, Polar Ice partnered with Polar Bears International in an effort to help save the polar bears. International Polar Bear Day is celebrated each year on February 27, so mark your calendars and raise a shot glass to these majestic creatures. To learn more and get involved, check out polarice.ca.

SPOTLIGHT: PARTY ANIMAL VODKA

Despite some bad vodka-animal juju, there are companies that spend time and money to ensure the safety and preservation of our four-legged friends. Party Animal Vodka believes in unleashing your inner party animal with a strong encouragement to "party with a conscience" on their website, where they list the organizations they donate profits to that protect the environment and benefit wildlife. Their partners at the time of this writing include humane societies, animal shelters, sanctuaries, and animal conservation organizations. Founded in Idaho, this company makes potato vodka from only locally sourced russet potatoes. Check them out for some Party Animal recipes at https://partyanimalvodka.com/cocktails/.

Peppermint Polar Bear Shots

Adapted from PolarIce.ca's Polar Bear Shooter recipe

Ingredients
½ ounce vodka
½ ounce white crème de cacao
½ ounce peppermint schnapps

Instructions
1. Grab a shot glass and combine schnapps, crème de cacao, and vodka for a smooth and minty shot that's sure to leave you refreshed and satisfied.

SPOTLIGHT: POLAR ICE

Polar Ice is a Canadian vodka company dedicated to providing high quality spirits made from the Arctic. Polar Ice is made from quality grains and the coldest Arctic water: they use a unique chill filtration process to produce water at 6° Celsius or 42.8° Fahrenheit. Their Ontario Peach flavor is sold exclusively in Canada, made with fresh peaches that grow along Lake Ontario for a smooth, natural taste.

VODKA IN THE MILITARY

Serving in one's military is a truly noble and admirable thing. I'm proud to be a military wife and serve my country as the support spouse. Fact or fiction, there are a wide range of stories from military men and women from around the world involving vodka (and various other liquors). After the Nazi's surprise invasion of Russia back in 1941, Joseph Stalin reinstated a national vodka ration for the Red Army. The ration had been previously discontinued by Czar Nicholas II back in World War I. According to Mark Schrad, author of *Vodka Politics,* Stalin's specific order was to give 28 million men one glass of vodka a day over the course of four years. Schrad estimates that ration would have amounted to over one billion liters of vodka every year. That's a lot of vodka!

The Army-Navy

Adapted from Sarah Sicard's patriot-inspired recipes at Task&Purpose.com

The Army-Navy football game calls for this drink to include gin instead of vodka. But hey, we're vodka snobs after all. Cheers! And may the best team win.

Ingredients
2 parts vodka
½ part lemon juice
¼ part Orgeat almond syrup

Instructions
1. Add all ingredients into a shaker with ice. Shake vigorously and strain into a chilled or frosted glass.

Liquid Courage

During World War II, Russian troops were issued small glasses of vodka just before their scheduled attacks. Some may scoff at the use of vodka to enhance courage in military troops, but as Ruslan Budnik writes for War History Online, it was usually consumed by young and inexperienced soldiers, and most think it more humane than the methamphetamines reported to be used by the Germans and other countries' militaries during that time.

Near Beer

The United States used to allow troops stationed inside of combat zones to drink near beer. Near beer is generally considered nonalcoholic but has around .4 percent alcohol by volume. Enterprising military service members would gather all of the near beer from across multiple camps and freeze it, which caused the pure ethanol to rise to the top. These promising chemists would then siphon off the pure liquor and discard the rest. This liquor may not technically be vodka, but it was close enough. Currently US forward-deployed military locations have only 0.0 percent abv beer, so the practice of freezing near beer has come to an end.

Alcohol Allowances

Not all countries ban alcohol for their troops like the United States, and some provide rationed amounts of various alcohols to their military service members. When an American military friend of Jay's was stationed on a British Naval ship at the end of the year 2000, he was afforded his choice of either three cans of beer, one glass of wine, or one shot of rum daily. But according to WarontheRocks.com, the practice of giving alcohol allowances to sailors ceased long ago. Black Tot Day, July 31, 1970, is marked as the day the British Navy stopped issuing its sailors a daily rum quota. But I suspect it still occurs, even if in secret.

We Ran Out

Since Russia holds firm to its creation rights to vodka, it is fitting that it is also credited with being the only country to run out of vodka. As World War II reached its bitter end, Nazi Germany finally ordered their troops to unconditionally surrender on May 7, 1945, and brought about a global sigh of relief. It took longer to share information in those days, so it was an hour after midnight on May 9, 1945, when a Russian radio host named Yuri Levitan announced the news of the German surrender on Radio Moscow.

Every country felt the weight of the Nazi war machine, but when the news of the surrender hit the airwaves in Moscow the people exploded into riotous celebration. Less than twenty-four hours later, when Joseph Stalin officially addressed the people, the Russians had already celebrated the nation free of all of its vodka.

I cannot speak to the level of relief they must have felt, but to empty Russia of its stores of vodka speaks volumes.

Frosted Black Russian

From Barbara Mealey's Potent Punches

Ingredients
1 ounce Kahlua
3 ounces vodka
3 ice cubes, crushed

Instructions
1. Combine Kahlua and vodka, add crushed ice, and serve in a small, chilled brandy snifter. Accompany with a cocktail straw.

Yield One serving

Korea

Before the Korean War, soju, the national drink of Korea, was distilled from rice. During the early 1950s, however, when the war was at full speed, rice was needed for food, and distilling from rice was made illegal in Korea. Not to be deterred, soju manufacturers began using other starches such as wheat, sweet potatoes, and tapioca. These are some of the same bases found in various vodkas around the world, and that makes sense, since Korea's soju is a neutral spirit akin to vodka. The main difference would be that soju has only half the alcohol vodka has, making it burn less and, according to Nick Hines of *Vinepair*, making it a better pairing for meals. In his article "Soju: Everything You Need to Know about Korea's National Drink," Hines makes a good case for every vodka snob giving this sweet, light, and neutral spirit a try.

Vietnam

Military service members stationed in and around Vietnam during the Vietnamese conflict were lucky enough to have US beer manufacturers who supportively shipped their brew across the globe, but excited and adventurous GIs who visited local nightlife establishments might find that the only vodka available was Vodka Hanoi. Vodka Hanoi is definitely not a premium vodka and was probably only there as a liquid nod to Russian diplomats and advisors. As Hannah Stephenson relates in her roundup of Vietnamese alcohol brands for *Culture Trip*, Vietnam is more of a beer kind of place. Nowadays an expat in Vietnam won't have to settle for beer or subpar vodka, though, thanks to the relatively new premium Kai Vodka, one of the few vodkas distilled from rice, which gives it subtle sweet notes.

Remembering the Fallen

Every year the men and women of the armed forces take at least one day to pay special tribute to their fallen comrades, brothers and sisters, and friends. Usually where there is a small gathering of those left standing, there is a toast: a shot of vodka in honor of those who have fallen, or, on some occasions, a drink poured in memory of a lost friend. This drink sits untouched until the gathering is concluded; then it is ceremoniously poured out in remembrance.

Another way military members are remembered is with a special table commonly found on military installations in the dining facilities. Reserved for the men and women who are no longer with us, the table is set for one and adorned with symbolic items, such as lemon slices, to represent the bitterness of their loss and salt to reflect the tears of their families. But the most poignant item is a glass set for the lost service member, inverted because this member cannot partake.

SPOTLIGHT: THE OFFICIAL SPIRIT OF A GRATEFUL NATION

With more than ten gold and silver medals in blind tasting competitions, Heroes Vodka deserves a place in *How to Be a Vodka Snob*'s spotlight. Even more deserving of respect than their quality flavor and high honors is the story behind the scenes.

In 2009, USMC veteran Travis McVey founded a company that would give back to organizations that invested in the lives of veterans as a way to honor the lost lives of those he loved. The first Heroes Vodka was bottled on a day that happens only once every century: November 11, 2011 (11/11/11). November 11 also happens to be Veterans Day.

Made from 100 percent American grain in Frankfort, Kentucky, Heroes Vodka is distilled four times. And unlike most premium vodkas, every purchase supports American heroes. So the next time you're at the liquor store, pick up a bottle and give thanks for those men and women who sacrifice for this great nation.

The Smoking Lamp

US Naval ships have what they call a smoking lamp. This largely metaphorical lamp is used to indicate that smoking is currently allowed or disallowed. Usually it is announced over the ship's intercom. "Attention, the ship is transferring JP8 [fuel]. The smoking lamp is out. No smoking forward of frame 54 until further notice."

When Jay was stationed out-of-state for reserve duty, his unit had a room designated as the "heritage room" which was adorned with all manner of things collected during years of military service and deployments. Two things were central in this room: first, a couch that had been re-covered with retired utility uniforms and patches and second, an old, ugly beige refrigerator. On top of this vintage appliance sat a leg lamp like the one from *A Christmas Story*. This was the drinking lamp. At the end of the workday on Sunday afternoons, the reserve unit commander would come in and turn on the drinking lamp to signify the end of the service members' drill weekend, as well as the opportunity to share a drink with friends before departing to their semi-normal lives for another month. The fridge held various beers, but it also held a bottle of vodka. Some military members preferred to share a quick shot with each other before parting ways.

Big Orange Sunrise

Adapted from a Heroes Vodka (@HeroesVodka) Instagram post

Ingredients
2 ounces Heroes Vodka
1 ounce Triple Sec
2 ounces fresh orange juice
Splash of lemon lime soda

Instructions
1. Pour all ingredients into a Collins glass and stir.
2. Garnish with a thin orange wedge.
3. Sip and enjoy!

SPOTLIGHT: VICTOR VODKA BY HOTEL TANGO ARTISAN DISTILLERY

United States Marine veteran Travis Barnes founded Hotel Tango Distillery with his wife Hilary in 2014. Travis was wounded and disabled during his third combat deployment. Hotel Tango comes from NATO's phonetic alphabet for the first letters in the names of founders—Hilary and Travis Barnes. Hotel Tango is inspired by Travis's military service, and the military connection is present in every aspect of their craft spirits.

They grow their fresh ingredients using sustainable methods, and their property also features a cocktail lounge, an event space, and a tasting room where you can sample the wide range of their offerings. Their Victor Vodka is distilled using 100 percent locally sourced Indiana corn to produce a clean, sweet vodka that you would be proud to serve. Check them out online at www.hoteltangowhiskey.com, or, if you are ever in the Indianapolis, Indiana, area check their hours and schedule a visit.

VODKA AND FOOD

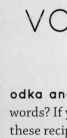

Vodka and food: Could there possibly be a sweeter combination of words? If you're looking for some amazing meals, look no further than these recipes, all of which call for vodka as a key ingredient. As we prepare to dig into some delicious dinners, we wanted to highlight some incredible midwestern vodka brands.

Square One Organic Vodka, North Dakota

SquareOneOrganicSpirits.com

Square One is an environmentally friendly company with the vision to create a certified organic fermentation process. This higher-priced vodka is worth the cost. Distilled from North Dakota rye and cut with waters originating in Wyoming's Teton Mountains, Square One Organic Vodka is worth every cent.

Glacial Lakes, South Dakota

GlacialLakesDistillery.com

The owners of Glacial Lakes Distillery have a simple, yet wise, motto: Follow Grandma's lead. Maintaining excellence through small batches, Glacial Lakes uses grains harvested from their own 160-acres or locally sourced from neighboring farms. In addition, the water used is uniquely filtered by deposits left from retreating glaciers. Their commitment to excellence is proven in the taste of their product: crisp and smooth.

Cooper's Chase, Nebraska

CoopersChase.com

The first federally and state-licensed distillery in Nebraska is Cooper's Chase, founded in 2009 after two partners sketched their dreams and ideas on a bar napkin. This vodka is especially close to my heart because I'm a born Cornhusker, and my father still roots for what he says will always be the best college football team in sports history.

Only the best grain is used in Cooper's Chase vodka, made in a 100-gallon hybrid still that looks like a pot but works like a column. Cooper's Chase is proud to have placed at the Denver International Spirit Competition and continues to be a company that loves and cares about its customers.

Valentine Vodka, Michigan

ValentineDistilling.com

Chosen as 2016's World's Best Vodka at the World Drinks Awards in London, Valentine is a blend of corn, barley, and wheat distilled in copper pots. If you participate in a tasting, be sure to note their bar. According to the Pure Michigan website, which lists Valentine Vodka as one of their "12 Spectacular Spirits from Michigan Distilleries," it's made from reclaimed construction materials taken from abandoned buildings in Detroit, as is much of the Valentine facility.

Rehorst Citrus Honey Vodka, Wisconsin

GreatLakesDistillery.com

Reviewed as a "damn fine citrus vodka," by the Spirits Review, Rehorst Citrus Honey Vodka uses real lemons and fresh honey from artisanal beekeepers who also believe that purer is better. With no additives, this vodka boasts top place among all citrus vodkas, many of which use artificial flavorings. This hand-crafted vodka won the Gold Medal in the 2009 San Francisco World Spirits Competition.

Milo Vodka, Kansas

OrneryBrotherDistilling.com

Ornery Brother Distilling is a true micro-distillery utilizing milo, or sorghum, in its vodka in the place of a more typical vodka base. With no sugar added, this vodka is gluten-free, smooth, and sippable straight out of the bottle. Pour over ice and you've got a glass of what fans call "amazing water." Kansas is the number one producer of milo, a grain that is high in protein and used primarily in Asia. This new twist on an old spirt makes Ornery Brothers a brand to keep an eye on.

Cardinal Sin, Missouri

StLDistillery.com

Multiple-award-winning Cardinal Sin Vodka (and its sister beverage Cardinal Sin Starka) are made from toasted two-row malted barley and created using a patent-pending pressurized filtration system. Their tagline is "Sin without remorse," but the taste is anything but sinful. Boasting a crisp, clean, and ultra-smooth taste, Cardinal Sin is a finely crafted artisanal vodka. Their Cardinal Sin Starka receives its beautiful amber color and incredible flavor profile from the Missouri White Oak Bourbon barrels in which it is aged.

Zone Vodka from Iowa Distilling, Iowa

Iowa Distilling Company utilizes cutting-edge ozone technology to create their rich Zone vodka, which has a subtle rye flavor. The beauty of the Iowa Distilling Company is their dedication to supporting their neighbors and using locally sourced grains.

Bluestem, Illinois

BluestemVodka.com

Bluestem Vodka is named after the state prairie grass of Illinois and Missouri. This distillery uses corn and reverse osmosis water to create their sweet liquor. They've dubbed their distillation process the "submarine process" due to the shape of their still. You can book a tour and tasting on their website, and while you're there, be sure to try their trademarked signature cocktail the Stemcell®, which boasts their Bluestem Vodka with pineapple and grape juice.

18 Vodka, Indiana

18vodka.com

Handcrafted from rye, this spirit is named 18 Vodka because it is distilled 18 times in their German hybrid copper pot still. The spirit is so smooth, you can drink it straight up, or, if you please, mix it in your favorite cocktail.

OYO, Ohio

MiddleWestSpirits.com

OYO's (oh-why-oh's) Original American Character Vodka® is made from local red winter wheat and other local ingredients that bring a distinctive . . . and award-winning . . . flavor to their flagship spirit. The flavor profile, according to their website, is vanilla caramel bonbon, fig preserves, and spice. This 34 times originally distilled, unfiltered vodka is sure to be a favorite at your next get-together or event.

Time to Eat!

Speaking of get-togethers and events, it's time to dig into some recipes containing the spirit of the day! In this chapter you'll find a few favorite recipes that are easy to whip up and oh so delicious. I recommend using a quality vodka in these recipes to really pull the flavor profiles.

Bloody Mary Soup

A well-mixed Bloody Mary can be one of the best drinks on this planet. Rich, spicy, and filling, it's the perfect way to start off a lazy weekend. Even if you're not in the mood for a drink, you can savor that Bloody Mary flavor in a refreshing soup.

Ingredients

2 28-ounce cans crushed tomatoes

1 white onion, diced

½ cup carrots, diced

½ cup celery, diced

2 cloves garlic, minced

1½ tablespoons Worcestershire sauce

4 cups vegetable broth

Optional To give the soup a zestier kick, some recipes call for 1–2 teaspoons Old Bay Seasoning or 2 teaspoons of grated horseradish.

Instructions

1. In a large pot, heat the olive oil until it shimmers.

2. Add your mirepoix (onions, celery, and carrots) and sauté until the veggies are softened.

3. Add garlic and stir for a couple more minutes.

4. Lower your heat and add tomatoes, Worcestershire sauce, and veggie broth. If you're using a spice like Old Bay or horseradish, add it in this step, too. Simmer about five minutes, stirring occasionally.

5. To get your soup creamy smooth, use an immersion blender directly inside the pot. If you don't have an immersion (hand) blender, you can blend the soup. Allow it to cool slightly and add to blender in small batches. Be sure to remember to cover the blender!

6. Serve soup with dollop of sour cream or grilled cheese or enjoy all on its own!

Martini Cheese Dip

Adapted from Theresa Sandoval's Dirty Martini Dip on JustAPinch.com

Martini Cheese Dip is a surefire hit for your guests. I'm not a fan of olives, so I leave a ramekin of chopped green olives near the dish so my guests can sprinkle some on top of their dip if they so choose. It's so good, you'll want to make it when it's just you relaxing on the couch with a drink in one hand and the remote in the other, #NetflixAndChill-style. The dirty little secret behind this dish: there's no vodka in it.

Ingredients

8-ounce package cream cheese, softened

1 tablespoon mayonnaise (be generous!)

⅛ teaspoon black pepper

1–2 minced garlic cloves, or ½ teaspoon minced garlic

¼ cup scallions, chopped

2–3 fresh jalapeños, seeded and chopped (or 1 4-ounce can of diced jalapeños)

Optional

8-ounce jar of green olives, drained and chopped—reserve juice

Instructions

1. Blend all ingredients in a medium-sized mixing bowl.

2. Let chill in refrigerator for one hour.

3. Spoon into serving dish and serve with crackers, crostini, or veggies.

Main Dishes

Vodka Pizza Sauce

Adapted from J. Kenji López-Alt's Vodka Pizza recipe at SeriousEats.com

This is a triple batch recipe, as in, you can make at least three pizzas with this sauce. If you only need a little bit, the sauce will last up to a week in the fridge, or you can freeze it. After tasting pizza vodka sauce, you may never go back to marinara again.

Ingredients

2 tablespoons extra virgin olive oil

4 teaspoons minced garlic

1 teaspoon dried oregano

½ teaspoon red pepper flakes

1 28-ounce can whole peeled tomatoes, roughly broken up by hand

1 cup heavy cream

⅓ cup vodka

Salt and pepper to taste

Instructions

1. Heat olive oil in a medium saucepan over medium heat.

2. When oil shimmers, add the herbs and spices: garlic, oregano, and pepper flakes.

3. Stir constantly until fragrant, about 1 minute.

4. Add tomatoes and bring to a boil, then reduce to a simmer.

5. Cook, stirring occasionally, until tomatoes are reduced by one quarter, about 20 minutes.

6. Add heavy cream and bring to a boil, then reduce to a simmer, and continue to cook until reduced again by one quarter, about 20 minutes longer.

7. Add vodka and cook for seven minutes.

8. Remove from heat and season to taste with salt and pepper.

Note For a smoother sauce: Let sauce cool and then, in batches, blend on low speed until completely smooth, about two minutes total. (If the sauce isn't blending well, raise the speed slowly). Strain through a fine mesh strainer into a medium bowl. Sauce can be stored in a sealed container in the refrigerator for up to one week or frozen.

Lemon-and-Vodka Seared Scallops

Adapted from Chowhound

It was Gordon Ramsey, the chef that everyone loves to hate, who made me curious to try scallops. In almost every *Hell's Kitchen* episode that I can remember, scallops were an appetizer, and he would fling the rubbery ones through the galley if they offended him in any way.

I had to try one. My chance came on a cruise ship, and let me tell you something—those scallops were delightful. They are now one of my favorite appetizers, and I hope that this recipe either makes you fall in love with these tasty little treats or makes you fall in love with them all over again.

Try these alone, with crusty bread, or over your favorite pasta. Bon appetit!

Ingredients

1 pound sea scallops

1 tablespoon plus 1 teaspoon olive oil

⅔ cup vodka

2 tablespoons heavy cream

1 tablespoon freshly squeezed lemon juice

1 teaspoon finely grated lemon zest

Optional 2 tablespoons finely chopped fresh tarragon leaves. (If tarragon isn't a flavor-profile you prefer, feel free to omit them.)

Instructions

1. Heat 1 tablespoon oil in a large frying pan over high heat.

2. Pat scallops dry with paper towels to remove moisture.

3. Toss gently with 1 teaspoon olive oil.

4. Season with salt and freshly ground black pepper.

5. When frying pan is heated, add scallops. Cook on each side until golden brown, about 4 minutes total. Do not flip scallops multiple times. Transfer to plate and reserve.

6. Remove pan from heat. Carefully add vodka, scrape up any browned bits from bottom of pan, and stir gently.

7. Return pan to medium-low heat and add cream, lemon juice, and lemon zest, stirring gently to incorporate.

8. Return scallops to pan and cook until heated through— about 2 minutes.

9. Garnish with tarragon, if desired, and serve.

Penne alla Vodka

Adapted from Cara Langer's recipe at Taste of Home

This dish is to die for and oh-so-easy to prepare. At its core, the sauce is a beautiful blend of acidic tomato sauce, rich heavy cream, vodka, and lush penne with onions and crushed red pepper. Vodka sauce is also known as pink sauce and can vary in its color vibrancy. Delish!

Ingredients

1 16-ounce package penne pasta

3 tablespoons butter

2 garlic cloves, minced

4 ounces thinly sliced prosciutto, cut into strips

1 28-ounce can whole plum tomatoes

¼ cup vodka

½ teaspoon salt

½ teaspoon crushed red pepper flakes

½ cup heavy whipping cream

½ cup shredded Parmesan cheese

Instructions

1. Cook pasta according to package directions.

2. While pasta boils, add butter to large skillet over medium-high heat.

3. When butter melts, add garlic and stir 1 minute.

4. Add prosciutto; cook 2 minutes.

5. While prosciutto cooks, drain and chop plum tomatoes.

6. Stir in tomatoes, vodka, salt, and pepper flakes, and bring to a boil.

7. Reduce heat; simmer, uncovered, for 5 minutes.

8. Stir in cream and stir occasionally for another 2–3 minutes.

9. Drain pasta.

10. Toss pasta and sauce and top with cheese.

Chicken Riggies

Adapted from GonnaWantSeconds.com

This dish is a favorite invented by Italian Americans in the Utica, New York, area. We're using sherry to marinate the chicken but bringing in the vodka for the sauce. While it has a similar profile to penne alla vodka, this dish will be sure to become a staple in your meal rotation.

Ingredients

Chicken

½ cup dry sherry

4 tablespoons olive oil, divided

3 cloves garlic, minced

2 teaspoons Italian seasoning

2 pounds boneless, skinless chicken breasts

Pasta

16 ounces rigatoni, uncooked

SAUCE

2 tablespoons butter

1 red bell pepper, diced

½ green bell pepper, diced

4 pickled hot cherry peppers, chopped

1 medium yellow onion, diced

4 cloves garlic, minced

¾ cup vodka

1 4-ounce can tomato paste

1 28-ounce can crushed tomatoes

¼ teaspoon salt

⅛ teaspoon black pepper

1½ cups heavy cream

8-ounce package cream cheese, cut into cubes and at room temperature

1½ cups parmesan cheese

Instructions

1. Combine sherry, 2 tablespoon olive oil, minced garlic, and Italian seasoning in a one-gallon resealable plastic bag.

2. Cut chicken into cubes and seal in bag. To prevent leaks, place bag in baking dish to marinate. Refrigerate 60 minutes.

3. After an hour, drain chicken and discard marinade.

4. Set a pot of water to boil. Once boiling, add rigatoni and cook following package directions.

5. Heat remaining 2 tablespoons olive oil in a large pot.

6. Cook chicken in batches, over medium-high heat. Spoon chicken onto plate or dish and set aside.

7. In the same pot, lower heat and melt butter.

8. Sauté onions, pepper, and garlic until soft, about 7–10 minutes.

9. Pour 1 cup vodka into pot and bring to a boil.

10. Add tomato paste, crushed tomatoes, cream cheese, salt, and pepper and bring back to a boil.

11. Reduce heat and simmer 8–10 minutes until mixture thickens slightly.

12. Add chicken.

13. Stir in cream.

14. Add chicken sauce mixture to drained pasta and fold in until pasta is coated.

15. Sprinkle with parmesan and serve.

Desserts

Ice Cream Cookie Sandwiches

This is going to be a super basic recipe. You can make two batches: one with vodka for you and one without vodka for your friends who don't partake or the kiddos— who are going to be begging for an ice cream sandwich on a hot day. If you live in Maryland, you can pick up a carton of Arctic Buzz ice cream which is pre-infused with vodka and, according to Madison Flager at Delish.com, boasts an 8.6–8.9 percent alcohol content by volume.

Ingredients

Cookies or graham crackers, totally your choice

1 pint (600 ml) of your favorite ice cream

3 fluid ounces (75 ml) of quality vodka

Optional fruit slices or berries

Instructions

1. Add ice cream and vodka to blender (and berries if using them).

2. Blend until smooth.

3. Pour into freezer-safe container and freeze for a minimum of six to eight hours.

4. Scoop ice cream onto a cookie or graham cracker and top with another cookie or graham cracker. Enjoy!

Vanilla Vodka-Infused Cherries, aka Drunken Cherries

One of my favorite memories is spending summers in Ohio with my aunt and grandparents. One evening, my aunt let me try a taste of her infused cherries. My mouth still waters remembering that sweet taste of amaretto and tart cherry. These vanilla vodka–infused cherries are next on my yummy treat list. May they bring back memories of farmhouse kitchens and fireflies for you as well.

Ingredients

1 14-ounce jar maraschino cherries or fresh cherries, as desired

Vanilla vodka of your choice

Instructions

If using a purchased jar of maraschino cherries:

1. Drain the juice from the cherry jar.

2. Add vanilla vodka to almost the top of the jar.

3. Cover and let sit on counter overnight.

4. Drain the vodka. Be sure to save it for shots or an addition to a Moscow Mule or other drink!

5. Gently pat cherries dry.

For fun If desired, dip the cherries in melted chocolate (make sure all the water is dried off so the chocolate doesn't seize) or frosting of your choice.

Please note Cherries will swell inside jar.

If using fresh cherries

If you want to use fresh cherries, follow directions above, but note that the soaking process can take a lot longer. According to Lisa at GarlicAndZest.com, drunken cherries made with fresh cherries can take up to six months to fully infuse! Lisa also fills the jars up about one third of the way with sugar and shakes to dissolve before preserving. And make sure to rotate the jars every week or so.

Note Fresh cherries will shrink to roughly half their size when boozed up.

Godiva Liqueur Brownies

Adapted from Teri Rasey's recipe at TasteofHome.com

There is nothing like the smell of freshly made brownies to fill a home with warmth. This decadent dessert deserves a spot in our *How to Be a Vodka Snob* recipe list for the sheer chocolate of it all. You had me at Godiva.

Ingredients

BROWNIES

¾ cup butter, softened

1 cup sugar

1 cup packed brown sugar

4 large eggs

½ cup Godiva Chocolate Liqueur

2 tablespoons chocolate vodka

2 tablespoons clear crème de cacao

1⅓ cups all-purpose flour

¾ cup baking cocoa

1 teaspoon baking powder

½ cup semisweet chocolate chips

GLAZE

1 cup confectioners' sugar

4 teaspoons butter, melted

2 tablespoons Godiva Chocolate Liqueur

1 tablespoon chocolate vodka

1 tablespoon clear crème de cacao

Instructions

BROWNIES

1. Preheat oven to 350° Fahrenheit. Spray 13×9–inch baking dish with cooking spray.

2. In large bowl, beat butter and sugars until light and fluffy.

3. Add eggs, one at a time, beating well after each addition. Add liqueur, vodka and crème de cacao until blended.

4. In separate bowl, whisk together flour, cocoa, and baking powder until well mixed. Stir in semisweet chocolate chips.

5. Fold chocolate chip mixture into butter mixture until combined.

6. Bake for 24–28 minutes, or until center is set. Let cool completely before cutting.

GLAZE

1. Mix all ingredients until smooth.

2. Once brownies are cooled, spread mixture over brownies.

3. Cut into squares and enjoy! If there are any extras, store in an airtight container.

Beef Kholodets (or Studen), aka Vodka's BFF

There is only one way to end a book on vodka and that is to end with a food that is apparently a Russian vodka-pairing staple. Kholodets is notably called "Vodka's best friend." However, after reading the ingredients and the instructions, I can safely say this recipe is not a friend I want to make. Upon reading the description, all I could think about were the horrible jello salads from the 1970s that kept their shape no matter what, even if the ingredients were cottage cheese and salmon. Not kidding. Beef Kholodets also includes meat and vegetables, and is served as either an appetizer or main course with horseradish or mustard on the side.

To those of you braver than I, here is the recipe for Beef Kholodets.

Ingredients

2 cow legs (shins)
1 small carrot, sliced
2 eggs, sliced
2–3 cloves of garlic
1–2 teaspoons of ground red pepper
1–2 teaspoons of salt

Instructions

1. Thoroughly clean cow legs with brush.
2. Boil cow legs.
3. Skim the foam layers. They will eventually change color from blackish-gray to white.
4. When there is no more foam, turn the heat to medium–low and cover the pot with a lid, but allow a small opening for steam to escape.

5. Boil until the meat is ready to come off the bone and the water turns a milky white (2–3 hours). **Note** Do not take the broth off the stove too early. The best method for testing the broth's readiness is to take a spoonful, let it cool and then smear it on your lips. If your lips momentarily stick together, you can be assured that your broth is ready.

6. Add salt. Be generous here. The vegetables will absorb the extra salt.

7. Place eggs and carrot slices into an aluminum pan.

8. Slice meat into bite-sized pieces and add to the aluminum tray. Add the bone marrow for more flavor.

9. Strain broth into another pot, separating it from the meat.

10. Add squeezed garlic cloves and red pepper to broth. Pour into aluminum tray and let cool.

11. Refrigerate for 24 hours. *Do not put into freezer*! The consistency should be a little firmer than Jello.

12. Cut into slices, garnish with parsley, and serve with a side of mustard or horseradish.

EPILOGUE

How to Be a Vodka Snob was a super fun book to write. I learned so much in the writing and research that my friends and family got tired of me spouting off little vodka facts and tidbits. Jay was thankful that we had the opportunity to pen these pages, though, because it meant lots of tastings and yummy bonus date nights.

It is my sincere wish that this book was a pleasure to read and that you enjoyed the fun facts, tested some recipes, and maybe tried a few new vodka brands. I definitely stretched myself beyond my tastebud comfort zone and found a true appreciation for artisanal, handcrafted vodkas from some of the smaller companies. I hope you will too.

I'd love to continue this vodka snob journey with you on social media. If you make one of the recipes, please tag me on Instagram (@brittanyjacquesauthor), and if you make any gorgeous cocktails of your own, I'd love to see those pics, too!

May you always be in good health and enjoy every sip.

Drink sophisticatedly, my friends.

Vashe zrodovye!

Selected Bibliography

I found so many fantastic recipes and stories and so much history about vodka during the research of the book. I've included some of my sources here so you can deep dive further into the awesome world of vodka!

Cookbooks

Foley, Ray. *The Vodka 1000: The Ultimate Collection of Vodka Cocktails, Recipes, Facts, and Resources*. Naperville, IL: Sourcebooks, 2007.

Mealey, Barbara. *Potent Punches: The Retro Guide to the Original Party Drink*. Bloomington, IN: Red Lightning Books, 2018.

Rose, John. *The Vodka Cookbook*. London: Kyle Cathie, 2005.

Sophia, Sarah. *Vodka Recipes: The Best Vodka Recipes from Around the World*. The Essential Kitchen Series. Scotts Valley, CA: CreateSpace, 2016.

Waller, Dennis. *Texas Jack's Famous "How to Make Infused Vodka" Recipe Book: Over 70 Simple to Make Recipes*. Scotts Valley, CA: CreateSpace, 2014.

Sources and Further Reading

Archibald, Anna. "Flavored Vodkas You Should Include for Your Next Happy Hour." *Thrillist*. Updated April 1, 2020. https://www.thrillist.com/spirits /vodka/best-flavored-vodka-brands-ranked.

Asimov, Eric. "A Tinge of Citrus in a Vodka Bottle." *New York Times*, April 30, 2008. https://www.nytimes.com/2008/04/30/dining/30spirits.html.

Augustine, Cindy. "Why Filtration Matters When Distilling Vodka." Liquor.com, August 16, 2016. https://www.liquor.com/articles/vodka-filtration/.

Budnik, Ruslan. "Doping for War—Russian Vodka and German Amphetamines in WWII." War History Online, August 13, 2018. https://www.warhistoryonline.com/history/russian-vodka-german-amphetamines.html.

Burns, Iain. "Dancing Bear Is Finally Rescued after Spending Her Life Being Forced to Perform with a Travelling Circus." *Daily Mail*, August 10, 2017. https://www.dailymail.co.uk/news/article-4778680/Ukraine-s-dancing-bear-rescued-travelling-circus.html.

Chilton, Charlotte. "Eleven Gluten-Free Vodka Brands to Make Your Cocktail Hour Choice Easier." *Town and Country Magazine*, April 5, 2019. https://www.townandcountrymag.com/leisure/drinks/g27010719/gluten-free-vodka-brands/.

Cooke, Emma. "Seventeen Cocktails Every *Game of Thrones* Lover Must Try." April 20, 2016. https://www.buzzfeed.com/emmacooke24/drink-like-a-khaleesi.

Difford, Simon. "French 75 Cocktail—Recipes and History." *Difford's Guide*. Accessed September 16, 2020. https://www.diffordsguide.com/encyclopedia/1267/cocktails/french-75-cocktail-recipes-and-history.

Dykstra, Chip. "Belvedere Unfiltered (Rare Diamond Rye) Vodka." *The Rum Howler Blog (A Website for Spirited Reviews)*, July 3, 2015. https://therumhowlerblog.com/vodka-reviews/bevedere-unfiltered-vodka/.

Farm Flavor. "Traditional Wassail." FarmFlavor.com. Accessed June 6, 2019. https://www.farmflavor.com/recipes/traditional-wassail/.

Felten, Eric (2007, June 9). "A Cock(tail) 'n' Bull Story." *Wall Street Journal*. Updated June 9, 2007. https://www.wsj.com/articles/SB118133789715129488.

Fenton, Crystal. "Differences between Potato Vodka and Grain Vodka." Accessed February 20, 2020. https://www.leaf.tv/articles/difference-between-potato-vodka-grain-vodka/.

Flager, Madison. "You Can Basically Get Drunk off This Vodka Ice Cream." *Delish*, September 30, 2017. https://www.delish.com/food-news/news/a55868/vodka-ice-cream/.

French, Alicia. "Peanut Butter and Jelly Cocktail Recipes." *SheKnows*, June 28, 2012. https://www.sheknows.com/food-and-recipes/articles/963568/peanut -butter-and-jelly-cocktail-recipes/.

Frost, Natasha. "How America Fell in Love with Vodka." *Gastro Obscura*, January 25, 2018. https://www.atlasobscura.com/articles/how-america-fell-in-love -with-vodka-smirnoff.

Gin Foundry. "Gimlet." September 9, 2013. https://www.ginfoundry.com/cocktail /gimlet-cocktail/.

Go Moscow Mule. "Secrets of Moscow Mule History." Accessed May 14, 2020. http://gomoscowmule.com/moscow-mule-secrets/.

Green Hope Organic Vodka, "What's in Your Vodka? Why Ingredients Matter." March 6, 2017. http://greenhopevodka.com/whats-in-your-vodka-why -ingredients-matter/.

Hines, Nick. "Soju: Everything You Need to Know About Korea's National Drink." *VinePair*, March 7, 2017. https://vinepair.com/articles/soju-koreas-national -drink.

Hunt, Kristin. "There's a Whole Fried Chicken on This Bloody Mary." *Thrillist*, August 11, 2014. https://www.thrillist.com/drink/nation/the-chicken-fried -bloody-beast-sobelman-s-debuts-bloody-mary-with-whole-fried-chicken.

Kitchen Daily. "The Difference between Ginger Ale and Ginger Beer." *Huffington Post*, Food and Drink, April 20, 2012. https://www.huffpost.com/entry/ginger -ale-vs-ginger-beer_n_1438420.

KosherEye. "Van Gogh Vodka." Accessed January 19, 2020. https://www .koshereye.com/koshereye-features/in-the-spotlight/3473-van-gogh-vodka .html#.X1kFfdZ71R1.

Leal, Jennifer. "These Are All Your Favorite Celebs' Signature Drinks." *Marie Claire*, November 11, 2015. https://www.marieclaire.com/food-cocktails/news /g3298/celebrity-signature-drinks/.

"Love for Local." Florida Cane Vodka. Accessed September 16, 2020. http://cane -vodka.com/love-for-local/

Macalester College Department of Russian Studies. "Vodka: 'The Bitter Stuff.'" Accessed February 20, 2020. https://www.macalester.edu/russian/about /resources/miscellany/vodka/.

McKee, Ryan. "The Ten Cocktails Every Entertainment Junkie Should Know." *Ask Men*, Top 10: Movie Drinks. Accessed June 9, 2020. https://www.askmen.com/top_10/entertainment/top-10-movie-drinks_4.html.

Michelle @ A Tipsy Giraffe. "The Rory Cocktail (a Gilmore Girls 'Martini')." November 19, 2016. https://www.atipsygiraffe.com/rory-cocktail-gilmore-girls-martini/.

Miller, Jeffrey. "The Prohibition-Era Origins of the Modern Craft Cocktail Movement." *The Conversation*, January 15, 2019. Updated January 16, 2020. https://theconversation.com/the-prohibition-era-origins-of-the-modern-craft-cocktail-movement-109623.

Mitenbuler, Reid. "What Are They Drinking on Mad Men?" *Serious Eats*, Drinking in History: The Stories and History Surrounding What We Sip, April 1, 2013. Updated September 11, 2020. https://drinks.seriouseats.com/2013/04/what-are-they-drinking-on-mad-men-booze-cocktails-sixties-history-what-don-draper-drinks.html.

Moscow Copper Co. "Our Story." Accessed May 14, 2020. https://moscowcopper.com/pages/our-story.

Moss, Walter G. *A History of Russia*. Vol. 2, *Since 1855*. 2nd ed. London: Anthem Press, 2005.

Munro, Cait. "The Birth, Death, and Inevitable Comeback of the Cosmo, SATC's Greatest Icon." *Refinery 29*, June 6, 2018. https://www.refinery29.com/en-us/2018/06/200515/sex-and-the-city-cosmopolitan-drink-popularity.

Nalewicki, Jennifer. "What Makes a Cocktail a Modern Classic?" *Tales of the Cocktail*, April 4, 2016. https://talesofthecocktail.org/in-depth/what-makes-cocktail-modern-classic/.

Newell, Sean. "Ukraine Solves Its Alcoholic Bear Problem Just in Time for Euro 2012 (Also, Ukraine Had a Problem with Alcoholic Bears)." *Deadspin*, Soccer. June 17, 2012. https://deadspin.com/ukraine-solves-its-alcoholic-bear-problem-just-in-time-5919074.

Reiter, Amy. "Why Alcohol Content Is Measure in 'Proof.'" The Food Network. Accessed June 3, 2019. https://www.foodnetwork.com/fn-dish/news/2017/07/why-alcohol-content-is-measured-in-proof.

Rosenberg, Josh. "Five 'The Office' Inspired Cocktails for Your Next Work Party." *Floor 8*, April 12, 2018. https://www.floor8.com/posts/9214–5-the-office -inspired-cocktails-for-your-next-work-party.

Rohsenow, Damaris J., Jonathan Howland, J. Todd Arnedt, Alissa B. Almeida, Jacey Greece, Sara Minsky, Carrie S. Kempler, and Suzanne Sales. *Alcoholism: Clinical and Experimental Research* 34, no. 3 (March 2010), 509–18. https:// onlinelibrary.wiley.com/doi/full/10.1111/j.1530–0277.2009.01116.x.

Scarano, Ross. "Ten Things Every Guy Should Know about Vodka" *Complex*, May 9, 2012. https://www.complex.com/pop-culture/2012/05/10-things-every -guy-should-know-about-vodka/.

Schrad, Marc Lawrence. *Vodka Politics: Alcohol, Autocracy, and the Secret History of the Russian State*. Oxford, UK: Oxford University Press, 2014.

Stephenson, Hannah. "10 Vietnamese Alcohol Brands You'll (Learn To) Love." *Culture Trip*, August 8, 2018. https://theculturetrip.com/asia/vietnam/articles /10-vietnamese-alcohol-brands-youll-learn-to-love/.

Team Tasting Table. "Beet-Infused Vodka Cocktail: Stick to Your Health Goals and Still Get a Buzz." *Tasting Table*, Clean(er) Eating Recipes. January 4, 2017. https://www.tastingtable.com/cook/recipes/beet-vodka-cocktail-recipe.

Thomson, Julie R. "Here's How 'Sex on the Beach' Actually Got Its Terrible Name." *Huffington Post*, July 20, 2017. https://www.huffpost.com/entry/sex -on-the-beach-cocktail_n_596f74dfe4b0a03aba86b779.

Tünaydin, Pelin. "Rescuing the Bears, Silencing the Bear Leaders: Bear Dancing in Historical Context and Its Abolition in Turkey." Master's thesis, Sabanci University, 2014. http://research.sabanciuniv.edu/34036/1/PelinTunaydin _10026959.pdf.

Wilkerson, May. "Bears Forced to Drink Alcohol to Entertain Diners at Russian Restaurant." The Fix. Accessed September 16, 2020. https://www.thefix.com /content/bears-forced-drink-alcohol-entertain-diners-russian-restaurant

Williams, Breanne. "The Taste of Florida," *Plant City Observer*, Neighbors, March 22, 2018. https://www.plantcityobserver.com/the-taste-of-florida/.

Index

Brittany Jacques
is the nom de plume of a husband-and-wife team who are
addicted to good food, great drinks, and college football
season. Although both are native midwesterners,
the duo hails from supposedly sunny (but
often rainy) Florida. Vodka is
their secret passion.